TRILBY JAMES

Trilby James read Drama at Bristol University before completing the three-year acting course at RADA. She graduated in 1990 and over the years has worked extensively as an actor in theatre, film and television. In 2000 she also began working as a freelance director and teacher at several leading drama schools including ALRA, Arts Educational Schools, Royal Central School of Speech and Drama, East 15, Mountview Academy of Theatre Arts, Manchester Metropolitan University and the Royal Academy of Dramatic Art where she is now an Associate Teacher. She continues to work across courses, directing third-year performances as well as teaching first and second-year students, MA students and running workshops for shorter programmes. She is a script reader and dramaturg for Kali Theatre Company and has directed several play-readings for their 'Talkback' seasons.

THE GOOD AUDITION GUIDES

132149

The Good Audition Guides

CONTEMPORARY DUOLOGUES: TWO MEN

edited and introduced by

TRILBY JAMES

NICK HERN BOOKS
London
www.nickhernbooks.co.uk

A NICK HERN BOOK

The Good Audition Guides:
Contemporary Duologues: Two Men
first published in Great Britain in 2017
by Nick Hern Books Limited
The Glasshouse, 49a Goldhawk Road, London W12 8QP

Introduction copyright © 2017 Trilby James
Copyright in this selection © 2017 Nick Hern Books Ltd

Designed and typeset by Nick Hern Books, London
Printed and bound by CPI Books (UK) Ltd

A CIP catalogue record for this book
is available from the British Library

ISBN 978 1 84842 533 0

MIX
Paper from
responsible sources
FSC
www.fsc.org   FSC® C020471

Contents

Introduction

☞ WHY DUOLOGUES?

Whether you are doing theatre studies at school, taking part in a youth theatre, at drama school (perhaps in your final year and looking for showcase material), or attending a professional acting workshop, the duologue will arguably provide the most intense form of character exploration and analysis. It will draw on all the essential skills of the actor – namely playing an objective, identifying obstacles, incorporating backstory, staying in the moment and listening. It is what any Stanislavsky-based acting technique is all about, and a well-crafted duologue will allow you to put all these elements into practice.*

The twenty-five duologues in this volume are from plays that have largely been written post-2000. With the odd exception the characters range in age from fourteen to forty. There is a wide variety of character types and styles of writing from which to choose. They are all drawn from the extensive list of new plays published by Nick Hern Books.

☞ CHOOSING YOUR DUOLOGUE

A good proportion of these duologues for two men are of a familial nature, some are between friends and some are of a romantic or sexual nature. Several of the duologues are ethnically or geographically specific, but the majority can be played in any accent and by any ethnicity. Similarly, out of context, some of the duologues can be played either younger or older than specified. Use your judgement and change place names or other references to suit your own purposes.

You will also find a good mix between the dramatic and the comic, the overtly political and the more playful. Some contain strong language and deal with adult themes. All

*Konstantin Stanislavsky (1863-1938) was a Russian theatre practitioner who developed a series of techniques in order to help the actor towards a more realistic portrayal of his character.

provide a particular challenge and represent the pressing interests of some of our leading playwrights.

☞ PREPARING YOUR DUOLOGUE

To understand the characters and the context in any one piece, you will need to read the whole play and to undertake all necessary research. Work with your scene partner to create detailed character histories and a backstory. Work out what it is that you want in the scene, where your characters are in agreement and where they are in conflict. Is there a power struggle? Ask yourselves what the scene is about (see below) and think about the story you wish to tell and why. The duologues in this volume concern themselves with the human condition. They explore our deepest longings, fears and needs. They pose complex questions about how we relate to each other and to the world around us. By engaging in the characters' psychology you will be able to reveal what lies at the heart of a scene.

☞ PERFORMING OR PRESENTING YOUR DUOLOGUE

As obvious as it may sound, remember that the playwright has written a *conversation*, so you will need to listen and to reply accordingly without preempting any outcome.

Allow yourself to be affected by what is said to you as you respond, and think about the effect you want to have on your partner. Stay in the moment and remain flexible and open to any impulses you or your partner might experience. The best kind of duologue is like an exciting tennis rally in which the audience are gripped, not knowing which way it will go. Several of the duologues in this volume are highly physical. Perhaps you will be working with a director who will have their own ideas about how to stage the scene. If you are working just the pair of you, think about how and where you will move in the space and what sort of physical dynamic there is between the characters. In some cases the writer has given a detailed description of what happens physically. Follow their stage directions and think of it as 'choreography' as you would a dance. Some of the writers use forward slashes (/) to indicate when the other character interrupts with their next speech.

☞ THE USE OF PROPS

Several of these duologues require the use of props. As far as you are able you will want to seek out items that are as close to the specified article/s as possible. Most actors enjoy working with props. The challenge of how to handle them during a scene, and the comic and dramatic possibilities they offer are all very much part of the actor's craft. Be sensitive to anything that you handle on stage. Is it an item of rare or precious value? Is it something that disgusts you? Is it something that is dangerous and might frighten you? If you cannot get the 'real' thing, use your imagination to endow the object with all the qualities of the original.

☞ TIMING/EDITING

For the most part, the duologues are the same length as they appear in the original playscript. Unless you are looking for showcase material, where you will be obliged to edit a scene to the standard one to three minutes, you will find it more useful to have the complete scene as it is written. Occasionally I have modified a duologue to make it flow more easily, and where a duologue is exceptionally long I have shortened it. In these cases, I have inserted this symbol [...] to show where a cut has been made.

☞ HOW TO USE THIS BOOK

For each duologue I have provided a list of the following:

☞ WHO   The characters' names, their ages, and where they come from. In many cases, the characters can be played either younger or older than in their original context. If a character's accent is not native to you, you may like to try playing it in your own accent. However, watch out for duologues that have been written with a strong dialect or idiom and where the essential rhythm of the piece needs to be maintained.

☞ WHERE   For the most part, this is specified in the text. However, you may prefer to change place names if you wish to transpose the scene to suit your own accent.

☞ WHEN   Most of the duologues in this volume are set in the present day. Some are historical. Read the whole play to make further decisions about the time of year it is, day of the week and the time of day.

☞ WHAT TO CONSIDER   This will include the style of the play, its themes and use of language, the characters' backstories and some indication about what happens next.

☞ WHAT THE CHARACTER WANTS   Objectives to play. Once you have learned your scene and have done all the necessary research and preparation, the only thing you should be actively playing is the 'What do I want?' or the 'What do I have to have?'

☞ WHAT THE SCENE IS ABOUT   It is important to think beyond what your character says and does to the wider implications of a scene. This will enable you to play the scene with intelligence, sensitivity and a greater understanding and awareness of what the play is trying to say.

*

These lists are suggestions only. When you become increasingly familiar with your duologue you will find you have opinions of your own; you may even find yourself in disagreement with my notes. Use this book as a springboard from which you will form your own opinions and ideas. My notes are by no means a substitute for reading the play or for thinking for yourself about the characters and their situations; they are rather a tool intended to help, to provoke and hopefully to inspire.

The Duologues

#aiww: The Arrest of Ai Weiwei

Howard Brenton

☞ **WHO** 'Sportsman', an interrogator, Chinese, and Ai Weiwei, conceptual artist, Chinese.

☞ **WHERE** A small narrow room in a Chinese prison.

☞ **WHEN** Spring 2011.

☞ **WHAT HAS JUST HAPPENED** On the 3rd April 2011, as he was about to board a plane for Taiwan, the world-famous Chinese artist Ai Weiwei was arrested at Beijing Airport. He was detained for a further eighty-one days, during which time he was regularly interrogated (before being released on bail, charged with tax evasion). In the following duologue, Ai Weiwei is being questioned by an official described in the play as 'Sportsman'.

☞ **WHAT TO CONSIDER**

- The play is based on *Hanging Man*, an account Ai Weiwei gave directly after his release from prison to British arts journalist Barnaby Martin. You may wish to read it.

- Read Howard Brenton's fascinating introduction to the play, in which he tells how he was approached to write the play at Ai Weiwei's request.

- Research the work and political activism of Ai Weiwei. Howard Brenton observes: 'So much conceptual work in the West is tediously egocentric, it is all "me me me". Ai Weiwei's work is not about himself, it is turned outwards toward other people, society and the world, it is all "us us us".' This tells us something about the generosity of the man, which you will need to capture in playing him.

- Ai Weiwei's bravery and strength of character. He has been unafraid to criticise China's oppressive regime and continues to fight for freedom of expression. The fact that he survived the eighty-one days without having been crushed is testament to his resilience.

- The 'Sportsman'. It is important that the interrogator is a fully rounded character. We may not agree with his beliefs, we may dismiss them as propaganda or indoctrination, but in playing him you will need to get behind the psyche of a man who believes that what he is doing is right, dutiful and good.

- The Sportsman is described as 'fit'. He wears jeans and a Manchester United football shirt.

- Their relationship. Brenton describes Ai Weiwei's encounters with his interrogators as a 'Stockholm syndrome in reverse': in other words, the captors become fascinated by their captive. Find the points in the duologue where the Sportsman becomes drawn to Ai Weiwei, where their debate about art or loyalty to the state is stimulating to him. You may like to play the duologue with the Sportsman really enjoying the discussion.

☞ WHAT SPORTSMAN WANTS

- To break Ai Weiwei.

- To protect China and the Communist Party.

- Power.

☞ WHAT AI WEIWEI WANTS

- To defend himself.

- To preserve his sanity.

- To prove to his captors that he has done nothing wrong. (Note the way in which he quotes Mao in order to further his argument.)

☞ WHAT THE SCENE IS ABOUT   Indoctrination versus freedom of expression, classicism versus modernity, art and what constitutes it, suppression, domination, frustration, fear of change.

☞ NB   This play offers a number of other duologues from which to choose.

SPORTSMAN. Right. Admit it.

AI WEIWEI. Admit what? […]

SPORTSMAN. 'I admit the sunflower-seed art is a scam.'

AI WEIWEI. I don't admit that!

SPORTSMAN. Why not? Aren't you pleased with yourself? Dumping millions of worthless seeds on London? Seeds made of clay, that can't even grow!

AI WEIWEI. It's what people make of them that matters…

SPORTSMAN. I tell you what this is, my friend. A great big fat international economic scam. A load of little bits of clay all over the floor, how can that be art?

AI WEIWEI. It's art or it's not art, I don't care.

SPORTSMAN. What? You say you are an artist and you don't care about art?

AI WEIWEI. What I care about is providing a new condition. For art.

SPORTSMAN. A new condition for you. More dollars, more euros!

AI WEIWEI. No, a new perspective, and from that angle to see something new…

SPORTSMAN. What view? What angle?

AI WEIWEI. A way of seeing the world, in a new way!

SPORTSMAN. This is gibberish.

AI WEIWEI. No.

SPORTSMAN. Prententious, arty nonsense.

AI WEIWEI. No! But it's not logical, not practical. This kind of art deals with people's lives, directly. It intervenes in life. Creativity is… is the power to reject the past, change the status quo, seek new potential…

SPORTSMAN. And how can a load of grey sunflower seeds piled up in a room do that? Art must be beautiful, what's beautiful about your crap?

AI WEIWEI. The beauty is in people…

SPORTSMAN. What do you know of the people, the masses? I tell you what the masses want from art workers! A good picture, a tree that looks like a tree, mountain, woman, something uplifting, not a load of bits of clay, smashed-up furniture in a room, people wandering about a foreign city!

AI WEIWEI. You're talking about the classical view of art.

SPORTSMAN. I am, and you piss all over it! And it's more than being a conman. You insult China.

AI WEIWEI. How do I that?

SPORTSMAN. You insult the Party!

AI WEIWEI. But how?

SPORTSMAN. With this!

He gives AI WEIWEI *a colour printout of the 'Study of Perspective' photograph in Tiananmen.*

In Tiananmen Square. Holding up your hand in a gesture to Mao's portrait over the Gate of Heavenly Peace. You are giving the finger to the Great Helmsman!

He makes the rude middle-finger gesture in AI WEIWEI's *face, holding the photograph in his other hand.*

AI WEIWEI. No, that's only part of a larger work called *Study in Perspective.*

SPORTSMAN. Don't take the piss, Weiwei. I may not be as rich as you, I may not be as clever, but I know when the piss is being taken!

AI WEIWEI. I'm not cleverer than you, we are all as clever as each other. That photograph is one of a series. There's one in front of St Marks in Venice, one in front of the Coliseum in Rome, there's one in Paris in front of the Eiffel Tower, there's even one in Washington in front of the White House… (*Holds up the middle finger of his free hand, puts it down.*) It's how artists judge perspective in paintings. And the point I'm making is… it doesn't work any more! The classical view is very limited. It can't really cope with today's life, or today's understanding of ourselves, or our universe. And art must cope with our life.

All of it. Even this, you and me in this room, it must cope with everything, else what is it? Meaningless pretty trees, pictures that mean nothing! And I want art that means... Everything!

A beat. [...]

SPORTSMAN (*to* AI WEIWEI). You are a conman.

AI WEIWEI. Please, please, understand. You can understand. Everyone can understand. [...]

SPORTSMAN. You blogged.

AI WEIWEI. Yes...

SPORTSMAN. You attack the Communist Party of China.

AI WEIWEI. I wrote many things on my blog, before you closed it down...

SPORTSMAN. But you have fouled the water, what you wrote has been read. (*Reads.*) 'This Government is the most unreliable, unacceptable government.' What does that mean?

AI WEIWEI. It means what it means.

SPORTSMAN. When you say 'this Government' what government do you mean?

AI WEIWEI. Careful, be careful, struggle in your mind to be careful. (*To* SPORTSMAN.) That is just the article, I wrote it that way. You have to just read the article.

SPORTSMAN. Why are you being so timid? Are you scared of us? You always say you are very open! Why can't you say very clearly what you meant by 'this Government'?

AI WEIWEI. If you don't understand the article, give it here, I'll rewrite it for you right now!

SPORTSMAN (*shouts*). Don't be clever with me! You are a pornographer and a criminal.

AI WEIWEI. Why do you suddenly say I am a pornographer?

SPORTSMAN. I've researched what you call your art, I've seen the filthy nude photos you took.

AI WEIWEI. Nude images are as old as art itself.

SPORTSMAN. So is pornography.

AI WEIWEI. The nude in art is about our humanity, the photos were about our humanity!

SPORTSMAN. You photographed your wife in Tiananmen Square, lifting up her skirt!

AI WEIWEI. That's just fun.

SPORTSMAN. Fun? Your wife showing her knickers? Little knickers too! You like me looking at your wife's little knickers? Like men looking? It's porn. It's publicity, all over the internet?

AI WEIWEI. It's life! Life!

SPORTSMAN. Porn and politics, your rubbish art, it's all the same to you, just a con, to make money!

AI WEIWEI. Why do you go back to the money all the time? If you have the evidence against me, why do we go through this? Why don't you just… throw me away?

SPORTSMAN. We can. We will. If you don't admit your crimes.

AI WEIWEI. What crimes? (*Shouts.*) What? What?

AI WEIWEI *is straining forward, pulling against the handcuffs.*

Dead still.

SPORTSMAN. We have watched you for one year, you know. We have twenty-one accounts of close engagement.

AI WEIWEI. Close…

SPORTSMAN. Meetings with hostile forces. Enemies of the state, Chinese and foreign.

AI WEIWEI. So why suddenly arrest me now?

SPORTSMAN *stares at him.*

Who has decided?

SPORTSMAN *hands him a paper.*

SPORTSMAN. Read that.

AI WEIWEI *takes the paper.*

AI WEIWEI r*eading.*

A beat.

You blogged that.

AI WEIWEI. Yes but…

SPORTSMAN. Do you wonder why your blog was closed down?

AI WEIWEI. It's free expression…

SPORTSMAN. It's state subversion. It attacks the Communist Party of China.

AI WEIWEI. Yes but…

SPORTSMAN. You curse the Party!

AI WEIWEI *staring at the blog.*

The sentence underlined. Read it.

A beat.

Read!

AI WEIWEI (*reads*). 'Fuck your mother, the Communist Party.'

SPORTSMAN. Again!

AI WEIWEI. 'Fuck your mother, the Communist Party.'

SPORTSMAN. Again!

AI WEIWEI. 'Fuck your mother, the Communist Party.'

SPORTSMAN. Again!

AI WEIWEI. Blogs are satire, I wrote fast, in heat…

SPORTSMAN. Again!

AI WEIWEI. It's the net, it's freedom, why should I not say anything I like, why not, I'm human!

SPORTSMAN. Again!

AI WEIWEI. Fuck your mother, the Communist Party, fuck you, fuck you all, fuck you!

He bursts into tears. The paper slides from his hand on to the floor.

He lowers his head.

SPORTSMAN. Yes. Yes. There we have it. Yes. That's it.

A beat. AI WEIWEI *looks up.*

AI WEIWEI. You say I am a hooligan, but you created me. Can't you see that?

SPORTSMAN. Nevertheless, Ai Weiwei, the blog is clear evidence of state subversion.

AI WEIWEI. It was in the moment. You can do that, live in the moment. You can, if you're free.

SPORTSMAN. Gibberish. But I think you are a little bit shocked.

A beat. […]

AI WEIWEI (*quoting*). 'It is necessary to investigate both the facts and the history of a problem in order to study and understand it.'

A beat.

SPORTSMAN. What?

AI WEIWEI (*quoting*). 'Marxist dialectical materialism, which demonstrates the constant struggle between opposites in an empirical setting, is the best method toward constant improvement. Objective analysis of problems based on empirical results is at a premium.'

SPORTSMAN. What are you talking about?

AI WEIWEI. I'm quoting Mao in his Little Red Book. He's right. Analyse China's problems, find a way forward, improve.

SPORTSMAN You know so much more than we do, it's so sad. (*Close to him.*) Weiwei, you won't survive what they do to you in prison. Two years and even if you're not dead, your mind will have gone. You will be destroyed.

2nd May 1997

Jack Thorne

☞ **WHO**   Jake and Will, both sixth-formers, aged eighteen.

☞ **WHERE**   Jake's bedroom.

☞ **WHEN**   7.37 a.m., 2nd May 1997.

☞ **WHAT HAS JUST HAPPENED**   Jake and Will, both eighteen, have been asleep in each other's arms. Jake is the first to wake. He goes to the bathroom, waking Will as he does so. Will gets up. He has an erection. Will gets back into bed, doing his best to conceal his erection. Jake returns to the bedroom with a stack of newspapers and an apple. Will pretends to be asleep. It is the morning after the election night in which Tony Blair led a landslide victory for the Labour Party. Despite the excitement, it is also a normal school day for which the boys must get ready. This scene comes at the end of a full-length play which has shown us two other couples earlier that night.

☞ **WHAT TO CONSIDER**

- It was hot in London that night and there was an atmosphere of shock and excitement as many high-profile Conservative politicians, including Michael Portillo, lost their seats.

- Jack and Will are politically motivated. At eighteen, they will have been able to vote for the first time in a general election.

- Having influence over the outcome has given the boys a rush that has fed into their sexual attraction to one another.

- Despite going to the same school, they are not from the same social class. Think about how you will explore this through accent and the boys' physicality.

- Will is much clearer about his feelings for Jake. Make a decision about whether Jake can't or won't reciprocate. Perhaps he is scared to admit to his feelings.

- Jake's line: 'I knew it was going to happen, but not like this…' followed by: 'Such a majority. Such a…' Make sure you capture the beat where Will assumes Jake is talking about the fact that they have slept together, only for Jake to backtrack and to make out that he was referring to the election results.

- Their choice of university. It is significant that the expectation for middle-class Jake to go to Cambridge is compared to that of working-class Will, who is looking to go to Leeds.

- The play was produced in 2009, over a decade later than the time of the play. The hopes and expectations of the new Labour Party to create a better world chimes with those of Jake and Will. The political disillusionment that followed points to the personal disappointment that Will, in particular, must face.

- The whole duologue is much longer than it appears here. You may wish to play the scene in its entirety or to edit it differently.

- Words in [square brackets] are there to indicate intention, and not to be spoken.

☞ WHAT JAKE WANTS

- To prove his intelligence

- To be 'top dog'. (Notice how competitive he is.)

- To distance himself from Will.

☞ WHAT WILL WANTS

- For Jake to love him back.

☞ WHAT THE SCENE IS ABOUT   The personal and the political, burgeoning sexuality, coming of age, hope, disappointment, the class divide.

☞ NB   This play offers a number of other duologues from which to choose.

JAKE *has a stack of newspapers. All the tabloids. And an apple. Which is green. He sits cross-legged on the floor. He starts flicking through.*

He stops at a page. He covers it over. He talks in a whisper.

JAKE. Jack Cunningham –

Jack Cunningham –

Jack Cunningham –

Jack Cunningham – […]

Cunningham Cunningham –

Richie Cunningham Richie Cunningham –

Jack in the box. Cunningham –

Richie Cunningham in a box. Richie Cunningham in a box. Richie Cunningham in a box. *Happy Days* are dead. Jack Cunningham.

WILL *opens his eyes and looks at* JAKE.

JAKE *covers the page over.*

WILL *closes his eyes again.*

Alistair Darling Alistair Darling –

Alistair Alistair Alistair –

He looks at WILL *again.*

He raises his voice slightly.

Darling Darling Darling –

Will you check the stairs, Darling?

I love you, Darling, will you check the stairs?

I love your stairs, Darling.

Darling Darling Darling, Will, are you awake?

WILL *says nothing.*

Will… because you're not making any noise at all, and normally, when people sleep,they make some noise, so are you awake?

Beat.

WILL *opens his eyes, thinks, and then closes them again.*

And then opens them.

WILL. Uh. Yeah.

JAKE. Did I… [wake you]?

WILL. No.

JAKE. How long have you been…?

WILL. I don't…

JAKE. Yeah?

WILL. How long since I made a noise? I mean, it's probably… I should make more… I'll remember that for next time…

JAKE. Yeah.

Beat.

Yeah.

WILL. What are you…?

JAKE. Remembering the cabinet. Memorising. Trying to. I figured Sharpey might… […]

WILL. Who've you got…?

JAKE. I'm starting with the… You heard about Frank Dobson?

WILL. No.

JAKE. Straight in. Health Secretary. They think.

WILL. Yeah?

JAKE. Yeah.

WILL. Wow.

JAKE. Yeah. Pretty huge.

WILL. I don't even know… where he came from…

JAKE. Select committees, I think. I mean, no… I don't know. It's a big promotion…

He looks for and reads.

Environment. He was environment. Shit. I should have…
[known] that. Which is now – I think, Prescott. Part of
Prescott's super ministry, have you? Oh. That's… […]

WILL. Wow.

JAKE. Yeah. Yeah.

Beat. WILL *thinks and then sits up.*

WILL. Did we – drink a lot last night?

JAKE. No. Not…

WILL. We didn't.

JAKE. No?

WILL. No.

JAKE. I mean, a bit… toasted a few in. Toasted a few out.
Lots of toast. With red jam on top.

WILL *smiles.*

WILL. I thought we…

JAKE. A bit.

WILL. Yeah. Because we didn't top-and-tail and that… In
bed, I mean…

JAKE. Yeah. Yeah. I wondered about that too.

WILL. Bladdered – probably –

JAKE. Yeah.

WILL. Frank Dobson.

JAKE. Yeah. For some reason I have no problem
remembering his name. Frank Dobson. Dobbing in Frank's
son. For some reason that's…

WILL (*laugh*). Dobbing in Frank – I'll remember…

JAKE. Dobbing in Frank's son. Yeah. Yeah. I'm all about the
memory – aids –

WILL *counts visibly under his breath – one, two, three – and
stands up. He looks down, his erection is no longer visible. He
looks up,* JAKE *is looking at him strangely.*

WILL. What?

JAKE. And we played that card game.

WILL. Yeah? Do you think Sharpey will test us?

JAKE. Yeah. I don't know. Maybe… 'Be prepared', though,
so… Dib–dib–dib.

WILL. Do you think I should…?

JAKE. I don't know.

Pause. JAKE *smiles.*

Oh, there's one you'll love – Dad bought me all the papers,
left them on the doormat before he –

WILL. Wow. I like the way he…

JAKE. Yeah. He's cool.

He knew I'd want all the papers. […]

– the *Star*'s all – 'It's a new Dawn – um, actually her name
is Gaynor.'

He searches through the stack and finds a copy of the Star. *It's
got a picture of a topless model on the front (she's Gaynor).*
WILL *laughs.*

WILL. Oh, that's really [funny] –

JAKE. Isn't it?

WILL. She's properly…

JAKE. I know.

WILL. Not really my [type] –

JAKE. No. Nor me. A bit…

WILL. Big.

JAKE. Yeah.

They both look at the picture again. Slightly scared.

Yeah. Big. Yeah. Well.

WILL. What did the *Guardian* say?

JAKE. Oh. He didn't buy that one, just the tabloids.

WILL. Right.

JAKE. I think he thought I'd just want the [tabloids], plus –
they are a bit cheaper than the…

WILL. Yeah. Still. My dad would never…

JAKE. Your dad's great. I love talking to your dad.

WILL. Yeah. He's…

JAKE. No. Seriously. He's great. He's brilliant. He can fix
things. My dad can literally fix nothing.

WILL. Yeah, that's – nothing's broken in my house.

JAKE. Well, nothing's broken in this house either. My dad
just gets someone in.

WILL. Yeah. […]

*JAKE gets some scissors and then sits on the floor and starts
cutting out articles for his scrapbook.*

JAKE. He left a note on the papers – 'Were you still up for
Portillo?' Which I thought was quite –

WILL. Yeah.

JAKE. He probably heard it on the radio but still…

WILL. We were.

JAKE. Yeah.

WILL. We were still up for Rifkind, actually. Was that before
or…?

JAKE. I can't remember.

WILL. We probably were still up when your dad got up to…
I mean, we can't have got more than two hours… three
hours…

JAKE. Yeah. I don't know when…

WILL. I don't feel tired.

JAKE. No?

WILL. No. Probably adrenalin. […]

JAKE. I bet Sharpey will make us do loads of stuff. […]

JAKE. You're going to have such a great time in Leeds.

WILL. Yeah? […]

JAKE. I really wanted to do that course.

WILL. Well, it's your reserve, though, so… […]

JAKE. Yeah.

WILL. If you don't get the grades…

JAKE. Yeah. But don't make it like that…

WILL. No. I –

JAKE. Because it's not. It's just, Cambridge is Cambridge, right? I mean, it just is…

WILL. Part of me hopes you don't get the grades. […]

JAKE. You know, I'd quite like it if we both ended up at the same [place] –

WILL. Yeah?

JAKE. University.

WILL. Yeah?

JAKE. We could do the first year in halls…

WILL. What [halls]?

JAKE. Student accommodation. Basically it means these huge blocks built by the –

WILL. Oh, I've seen those. Yeah. Halls of residence. I get what you're… Just call them… abbreviate them to 'halls', do they? I don't know much about – accommodation…

JAKE. That's because neither of your parents went to university.

WILL. Yeah. Probably. I mean, I know some stuff…

JAKE. First year in halls, and then we could get a flat or something in our second year.

WILL. Okay. Yeah. That sounds [great].

JAKE. I mean, it's not a problem, your parents having not gone to university.

WILL. No. I know.

JAKE. You're exactly what the Party is all about, frankly. You're the reason I'm pleased Dad couldn't afford to send me to private school.

WILL. Yeah.

JAKE. And sometimes we could go out into Leeds and try and pull or whatever and sometimes we could stay in. And you know, that year-abroad thing could be…

WILL. In America.

JAKE. Exactly. Maybe I should reject Cambridge if I get in…

WILL. Yeah?

JAKE. No. Probably –

WILL. No.

Pause.

JAKE. We just got to concentrate on getting that second term – I mean, with this mandate – but still… it could…

WILL. Yeah.

JAKE. But if we concentrate, if we keep moving forward, if we stick to our promises, we could –

WILL. Yeah. […]

JAKE. Will…

WILL. Yeah.

JAKE. Can you believe it?

WILL. No.

JAKE. We crushed them. […]

Seven Cabinet Ministers gone. Half their fucking seats. 418 seats.

WILL. It's amazing.

JAKE. I feel like I can do anything.

WILL. You can. You will. I mean, definitely.

JAKE *thinks and then moves to hug* WILL. *They hesitate a moment and then they hug.* JAKE's *back is towards us, but we see* WILL's *face really clearly. He's concentrating really hard on not getting an erection.*

Then he smells JAKE's *hair and can't help himself.*

JAKE *dislocates.*

He looks at WILL *for a moment. And then* JAKE *kisses* WILL *on the mouth. Just a peck but a significant one at that. They hold for a moment.*

As he breaks off, JAKE *smiles like he's done* WILL *a huge favour. And* WILL *smiles because, well…*

JAKE. I knew it was going to happen, but not like this…

WILL *tries to digest what just happened.*

WILL. No.

He smiles. And then he doesn't. JAKE *is watching him so-so carefully, but he's not showing it.* WILL *knows everything.*

JAKE. Such a majority. Such a…

WILL. Yeah. Jake –

JAKE. It's brilliant. It's like everything's new. I'm so excited.

WILL. Yeah? Jake –

JAKE. What?

WILL *takes a sniff and then a breath.*

He opens his mouth to speak. JAKE *turns to look at him.*

Spit it out.

WILL *says nothing.* JAKE *laughs.*

As the bishop said to the choirboy.

WILL. I – um – come to – come to Leeds with me –
JAKE. What?

WILL *thinks how to say it differently; he can't.*

WILL. Come to Leeds.

JAKE *looks at* WILL *closely.* WILL *swallows.*

JAKE. I can't. I'd be – betraying – myself.

WILL. Okay. Okay.

Beat. WILL *nods. Then nods again.* JAKE *just keeps looking at him.*

Remember I asked, though, won't you?

The Boy in the Striped Pyjamas

From the book by John Boyne
Adapted by Angus Jackson

☞ **WHO**   Bruno, German, and Shmuel, a Polish Jew, both nine years old. Both characters could be played by older actors.

☞ **WHERE**   Opposite sides of the fence separating the concentration camp at Auschwitz from the outside world.

☞ **WHEN**   1943.

☞ **WHAT HAS JUST HAPPENED**   Set against the backdrop of the Second World War and the Nazis programme of genocide directed against the Jews, the play tells the story of nine-year-old Bruno, whose father is promoted to Commandant and assigned to the concentration camp at Auschwitz where he is in charge of operations. For Bruno this means a move from his home and friends in Berlin where he was happy and free. Here at Auschwitz he is not allowed to go out, and he has no one to play with. Then one day from the window of his upstairs bedroom he spies the huts of the camp. Curious, he secretly leaves the house and, making his way through the undergrowth, arrives at the fence that separates the camp from the outside world. Here he meets Shmuel, who is a prisoner in the camp. As we see in the duologue that follows, Bruno has no idea about the true nature of Shmuel's situation and of his own father's work.

☞ **WHAT TO CONSIDER**

- The real-life history that surrounds this story. Take time to research the Nazis programme of genocide and in particular what they termed 'The Final Solution'.

- This stage version is based on the book by John Boyne. There is also a film version. You may like to read the book and watch the film in order to imagine the story more fully.

- Crucial to the story is Bruno's ignorance of what is really happening. When he refers to 'the Fury' what he really means is Hitler's title – 'The Führer'. Throughout the play he calls where they live 'Out-With', which from his lips becomes an innocent term for the infamous death camp at Auschwitz.

- Read the play to discover the dark twist at the end.

☞ **WHAT BRUNO WANTS**

- A friend to play with.
- Relief from his loneliness. (Notice the way he likes to make favourable comparisons between him and Shmuel. He is desperate for a playmate.)

☞ **WHAT SHMUEL WANTS**

- To be on Bruno's side of the fence.

☞ **WHAT THE SCENE IS ABOUT**   What happened to the Jews – how they were rounded up and transported, the effect of war on innocent people and children in particular, how as human beings we are more alike than we are different.

☞ **NB**   This play offers a number of other duologues from which to choose.

A huge fence cuts the stage across the middle. A small boy [SHMUEL] *is sitting cross-legged, looking through the fence. The two boys* [BRUNO *and* SHMUEL] *look at each other for quite some time.* […]

BRUNO. Hello.

Beat.

SHMUEL. Hello.

BRUNO. I've been exploring.

SHMUEL. Have you?

BRUNO. Yes, for almost two hours now.

SHMUEL. Have you found anything?

Pause.

BRUNO. Very little.

SHMUEL. Nothing at all?

Beat.

BRUNO. I found you.

BRUNO *takes a step in towards the fence, a beat later*
SHMUEL *unconsciously does the same thing.*

I live in the house on this side of the fence.

SHMUEL. Do you?

BRUNO. My room is on the first floor. I'm Bruno by the way.

SHMUEL. I'm Shmuel.

BRUNO. What did you say your name was?

SHMUEL. Shmuel. What did you say *your* name was?

BRUNO. Bruno.

SHMUEL. I've never heard of that name.

BRUNO. And I've never heard of your name. Shmuel.
(*Pause.*) Shmuel. I like the way it sounds when I say it.
Shmuel. It sounds like the wind blowing.

SHMUEL. Bruno. Yes, I think I like your name too. It sounds
like someone who's rubbing their arms to keep warm.

BRUNO. I've never met anyone called Shmuel before.

SHMUEL. There are dozens of Shmuels on this side of the
fence. I wish I had a name all of my own.

BRUNO. I've never met anyone else called Bruno apart from
me. I think I might be the only one.

SHMUEL. Then you're lucky.

BRUNO. I suppose I am. How old are you?

SHMUEL *sits*, BRUNO *sits too.*

SHMUEL (*sort of counting on his fingers*). I'm nine. My
birthday is April the fifteenth nineteen thirty-four.

BRUNO. What did you say?

SHMUEL. I said my birthday is April the fifteenth nineteen
thirty-four.

BRUNO (*wide-eyed and open-mouthed*). I don't believe it!

SHMUEL. Why not?

BRUNO. No. I don't mean I don't believe *you*. But I'm surprised because *my* birthday is April the fifteenth too. And *I* was born in nineteen thirty-four. We were born on the same day.

SHMUEL. I don't think I've ever met anyone with the same birthday as me before.

BRUNO. We're like twins.

SHMUEL. A little bit.

BRUNO *crosses his legs,* SHMUEL *does the same thing.*

BRUNO (*cocking his head to one side*). Do you have many friends?

SHMUEL. Oh, yes. Well, sort of.

BRUNO. *Close* friends?

SHMUEL. Well, not very close. But there are a lot of us – boys our age, I mean – on this side of the fence.

BRUNO. It's so unfair. Why do I have to be stuck over here on this side of the fence where there's no one to play with and you get to have dozens of friends?

SHMUEL. Where did you come from?

BRUNO. Berlin.

SHMUEL. Where's that?

Pause.

BRUNO. It's in Germany, of course. Don't you come from Germany?

SHMUEL. No, I'm from Poland.

BRUNO. Then why do you speak German?

SHMUEL. You said hello in German so I answered in German. Can you speak Polish?

BRUNO. No. (*Laughs.*) I don't know anyone our age who can speak two languages.

SHMUEL. Mama is a teacher in my school and she taught me German. She said she'd teach me English one day because I might need to know it.

BRUNO. Poland. That's not as good as Germany, is it?

SHMUEL. Why isn't it?

BRUNO. Well, because Germany is the greatest of all countries. (*Beat.*) We're superior. (*Beat.*) Where is Poland anyway?

SHMUEL. We're in Poland. This is Poland.

BRUNO. Is it? I don't think so.

SHMUEL. Yes it is.

BRUNO. Are you sure?

SHMUEL. Yes, I'm sure it's Poland, though not a very nice part of it.

BRUNO. No.

SHMUEL. Where I come from is much nicer.

BRUNO. Do you like exploring?

SHMUEL. I've never really done any.

BRUNO. I'm going to be an explorer when I grow up. The thing about exploring is that you have to know whether what you've found is worth finding. Sometimes when you explore you find something interesting, minding its own business, waiting to be discovered, like America. (*Beat.*) Other times you find things that are best left alone. Like a dead mouse at the back of a cupboard.

Beat.

SHMUEL. Which am I?

Beat.

BRUNO. You're America. (*Pause.*) Can I ask you something?

SHMUEL. Yes.

BRUNO. Why are there so many people on that side of the fence? And what are you all doing there? […]

SHMUEL. All I know is this. Before we came here I lived with my mother and father and my brother in a small flat above a shop. (*Beat*.) Every morning we ate our breakfast together and when we went to school, Papa mended the watches that people brought to him. (*Beat*.) I had a beautiful watch that he gave me, but I don't have it any more. It had a golden face and I wound it up every night.

BRUNO. What happened to it?

SHMUEL. They took it from me.

BRUNO. Who?

SHMUEL. The soldiers, of course. (*Beat*.) One day things started to change. I came home from school and Mama was making armbands for us from a special cloth and drawing a star on each one. [...] And every time we left the house, she told us we had to wear one of the armbands.

BRUNO. My father wears one too. On his uniform. It's very nice. It's bright red with a black-and-white design on it, like a cross but with extra bits. [...]

SHMUEL. Yes, but they are different, aren't they?

BRUNO. No one's ever given me an armband.

SHMUEL. But I never asked to wear one.

BRUNO. I think I'd quite like one. [...]

SHMUEL. We wore the armbands for a few months, and then Mama said we couldn't live in our house any more –

BRUNO. That happened to me too! The Fury came for dinner, you see, with a woman, and the next thing I knew we'd moved here. Did he come to your house and do the same thing?

SHMUEL. No, but then we were told we had to move to a different part of Cracow, where the soldiers built a big wall and we all had to live in one room.

BRUNO. All of you? In one room?

SHMUEL. And not just us. There was another family and they were always fighting with each other.

BRUNO. You can't have all lived in the one room.

SHMUEL. All of us. Eleven in total.

BRUNO *is sceptical.*

It was impossible to sleep. And there was a boy who kept hitting me even when I did nothing wrong.

BRUNO. Gretel hits me sometimes. She's my sister. And a Hopeless Case. But soon I'll be bigger and stronger than she is.

SHMUEL. Then one day the soldiers all came and told everyone to leave the houses. (*Beat.*) They took us to a train and the train… (*Bites his lip.*) The train was horrible. There were too many of us in the carriages for one thing. And there was no air to breathe.

BRUNO. That's because you all crowded on to one train. When we came here there was another one on the other side of the platform but no one seemed to see it.

SHMUEL. I don't think we would have been allowed on that one. We weren't able to get out of our carriage.

BRUNO. The doors were at the end.

SHMUEL. There weren't any doors.

BRUNO. Of course there were doors. They're at the end. Just past the buffet section.

SHMUEL. There weren't any doors. If there had been, we would all have got off.

BRUNO *mumbles under his breath.*

When the train finally stopped we were in a very cold place and we all had to walk here.

BRUNO. We had a car.

SHMUEL. And Mama was taken away from us, and Papa and my brother and I were put into the huts over there and that's where we've been ever since.

BRUNO. Very much like what happened to me.

The boys sit opposite each other like a mirror.

Boys

Ella Hickson

☞ **WHO**   Flatmates, Cam and Benny, aged about twenty-one.

☞ **WHERE**   The kitchen of their student flat, Edinburgh.

☞ **WHEN**   Present day. Summer.

☞ **WHAT HAS JUST HAPPENED**   It is the end of term and the end of their time at university for most of the characters in the play. Moreover, the contract is up on the flat that Benny and Cam share with two others. In anticipation the boys have been partying, and when the play opens it is the morning after the night before. Benny, who is about to graduate, has found refuge on top of the fridge and is enjoying a quiet moment alone before the partying continues. Cam, who is a virtuoso violinist, is nervous about an extremely important concert he will be playing at later that night. It could make or break his career. In the duologue that follows, Cam enters and confesses to Benny that he is terrified and that a large part of him does not want to perform.

☞ **WHAT TO CONSIDER**

- When he was ten years old, Cam's mother inadvertently lied about his age. The deception continued. He now says he is nineteen, when in fact he is twenty-one. In the competitive world of serious music, this two-year difference ensures that Cam retains his 'prodigy' status. To what extent does this feed Cam's feeling that the whole 'virtuoso violinist thing' is a sham, not of his choosing and that he wants out?

- In a dark twist to the story this is strangely resolved. Read the play to find out what happens next.

- Benny's brother (who was also part of the flat-share) has recently committed suicide. He hanged himself in the kitchen and his memory looms large.

- Why Benny is sitting on top of the fridge. He says he feels more in control up there. How might this be related to the death of his brother? Is it possible that by sitting high up he can imagine his brother's last moments as he prepared to hang himself and therefore feels closer to him?

- To what extent does the loss of his brother make him even more protective towards Cam?

- To what extent does his brother's suicide contribute to Benny's agnosticism?

- It is an unusually hot summer, and a local strike means the dustbins have not been cleared. The smell of rotting rubbish pervades the scenes.

☞ WHAT CAM WANTS

- Permission to fail.

- The freedom to choose for himself.

- Reassurance.

☞ WHAT BENNY WANTS

- To protect Cam.

- To make up for the loss of his brother. (He wasn't able to help his brother, but seems determined to 'save' Cam from himself.)

☞ **WHAT THE SCENE IS ABOUT**   Making sense of life's uncertainties and confusions, grappling with adulthood, the transition from boy to man.

☞ **NB**   This play offers a number of other duologues from which to choose.

CAM *takes a pill out of his pocket and places it in the palm of his hand he looks at it – he is on the verge of taking it...*

BENNY. What you doing?

CAM. Fuck, Benny, you scared the shit out of me.

BENNY. Shouldn't you be off by now?

CAM. My palms are sweating – my fucking /

BENNY. Don't take that.

CAM. My room's too fucking hot; Mack's playing his music

full fucking volume – outside everyone's in the sun, having a great time –

BENNY. Go to the college or the concert hall – they'll be quiet.

CAM. Stinks of fucking rubbish everywhere.

BENNY. You alright, Cam?

CAM. You'll all be having a party whilst I'm gone; getting the beers in.

BENNY. And you'll be making history.

CAM. All I can see out my window is fucking students – throwing flour and eggs all over each other. You seen how warm it is out there?

BENNY. You should go, mate, you don't want to miss it.

Beat.

CAM. Don't I?

Beat.

BENNY. Course you don't.

CAM. You just jump through the hoops and it works out – exams, degree – job – there's a path. There's no maybe – maybe not – or tonight's the fucking night. All on one moment, all on one person – fucking...

BENNY. You've got instructions.

CAM. What?

BENNY. The music – that's instructions, isn't it. Don't get that in an exam. (*Beat.*) Nice up here – like being above everything – you can control it, calmer – cooler somehow.

CAM. Cooler?

BENNY. Yeah.

CAM. You're on top of a fucking fridge, Benny.

BENNY. The top of a fridge is actually... I thought you were meant to be leaving?

CAM. I'll go in a minute.

BENNY. You're going to be late.

CAM. I've got ages. You want a drink?

BENNY. No thanks.

CAM. Come on – have a drink?

BENNY. I'm alright.

> CAM *picks up a ball and chucks it at* BENNY, BENNY *catches it.*

CAM. Come on – we'll chuck it about a bit? It'll help me calm down.

BENNY. What time are you meant to be there?

CAM. Don't know.

BENNY. Cam?

CAM (*snaps*). What?

BENNY. Go.

> BENNY *throws the ball back.*

CAM. It's easy for you – you've got a piece of paper saying you know it and that's that. Imagine if tonight I could just walk on stage and in front of that whole fucking crowd and just roll out a piece of paper and go – look – this says I can do it so there we go. And then everyone cheers and claps.

BENNY. It's just pressure – there's always going to be /

CAM. Exactly fucking right – it's always going to be there.

BENNY. You don't get to be excellent without there being pressure. It's a pay-off.

CAM. Who says I want to be excellent?

BENNY. Fifteen years of eight hours' practice a day.

> *Beat.*

CAM. There's this guy coming, tonight – he's a Russian virtuoso called Viktashev; he's come up from London. He's pretty much it – you know? The big balls.

BENNY. Nice.

CAM. And he sends me this email the other day – it's like two pages long, saying he's heard my stuff and how now is a vital time for me. How there's this competition in Belgium; it's called the Queen Elizabeth and it's, you know –

BENNY. The big balls.

CAM. Aye – and this Viktashev guy won it when he was nineteen, youngest ever – and he wants me to go and break his title. He says he's going to ship me over to Vienna and train me – just me and him. And he keeps going on and on about how there's this window, this right age – and if you can get through it – you'll go somewhere great but if you miss it – you won't get it back.

BENNY. You got to not listen to all that /

CAM. And then at the end he writes this little story about how the lowliest and youngest inmates in Russian prisons tattoo stars on their knees.

BENNY. Why?

CAM. To say they won't kneel to anyone.

BENNY. Bit much that.

CAM. I'm meant to do what he tells me and not do what anyone tells me – you know what I mean?

BENNY. Yeah, it's a bit much. Got to do it for you I guess.

CAM. If I was doing it for me I'd stay here and have a pint with you.

BENNY. Right. (*Beat.*) Can't waste it though, Cam.

CAM. Why not? My choice, isn't it?

BENNY. Right now I reckon I know more than I ever will again. Iteration, deconstruction, reification, homogeneity /

CAM. Show-off.

BENNY. I'm never going to use those words ever again. So I might as well not know 'em. It's a waste. You though, you'll go on getting better and better and you could be – great, you know? Like – really really get to the top of something – get close to – inch of God.

CAM. What?

BENNY. That's what my dad used to call it, 'inch of God', the extra inch that takes you from great to – really being the dog's fucking bollocks. You got a shot at that. Not to be sniffed at.

CAM. Don't sniff at the dog's bollocks?

BENNY. Do not, Cameron.

CAM. You can keep learning words – keep studying.

BENNY. Thanks.

CAM. PhD – teach or something.

BENNY. It's all criticism though… not sure that's something you want to be great at, is it?

CAM. Come up with your own ideas can't you?

BENNY. What's the point in following something hardly anyone else can follow? I reckon you just end up somewhere no one else is ever going to visit.

CAM. Hardly anyone is great at the violin.

BENNY. But everyone's got ears.

CAM. I don't want to do it.

BENNY. You have to.

CAM. I don't want to.

BENNY. I don't know if that really matters.

CAM. What?

BENNY. Bigger than you somehow; maybe.

CAM. It's my fucking fingers.

BENNY. You believe in God, Cam?

CAM. No.

BENNY. Not even in primary, like nativities.

CAM. Snow.

BENNY. What?

CAM. Imagine, a bit of snow right now – how good would that be?

BENNY. There's no snow in the nativity.

CAM. It's about Christmas.

BENNY. It's Bethlehem, it's red.

CAM. Alright, God squad.

BENNY. That's just geography. I miss it sometimes.

CAM. Geography?

BENNY. The idea of something above you. I used to imagine him just sitting up there at night-time, made you feel a bit safer.

CAM. You don't believe in him any more?

BENNY. Don't think so.

CAM. Why not?

BENNY. Learnt too much, I guess.

CAM. Can't you just decide?

BENNY. It's like you get two books by well-known people, credible people, out the library and they say opposite things but they're both meant to be right. What are you meant to do about that?

CAM. Choose one.

BENNY. Just like that?

CAM. Yeah – why not?

BENNY. Then you always know you chose it, so it's just a choice rather than a knowing.

CAM. What's the difference?

BENNY. You chose it – so you know can just un-choose it – flimsy. It's one option but it could have just as much been the other one, it's like TVs inside TVs – they eat each other – like all the facts sort of chase each other, round and round – all the articles and books and blogs and papers and

journals and they just keep running round and round and –
You remember *Little Black Sambo* –

CAM. Sounds a wee bit /

BENNY. It is – but that's not the point. It's this story where
this little kid meets these tigers and he gives them all his
best most colourful clothes so that they won't eat him and
they like those fancy clothes so much they chase and chase
each other so hard that they just melt into butter.

CAM. Tigers turn into butter?

BENNY. I guess I just miss – you remember when you had a
question, any question easy or hard, you know – what's
ham through to why are we alive – and you knew the
absolute best place to get a right answer was your dad.

CAM. Yeah.

BENNY. When your dad was like Google but better and with
hugs. (*Beat.*) You'll be alright. You've got to go though, you
got to try – it matters.

CAM. Can't I choose not to.

BENNY. You've got to go – one of us – has fucking got to – I
won't let you give up. I won't let this flat make you give up.

Pause.

CAM. I'm sorry, Benny.

BENNY. I just think you should try, that's all.

Beat.

CAM. But what if I do?

BENNY. What? What if you try? Then you'll know you did
your best.

CAM. Exactly.

Pause.

BENNY. You're going to miss it.

CAM. Sometimes think I'd be much happier if I'd never
picked the fucking thing up.

CAM *picks up his violin and starts to pack it away,* BENNY *watches silently.*

BENNY. Knock 'em dead?

CAM *nods.*

BENNY *nods.*

The Crocodile

Tom Basden
After Fyodor Dostoyevsky

☞ **WHO**   Ivan, a jobbing actor, thirties, and his best friend Zack, also in his thirties.

☞ **WHERE**   A zoo in St Petersburg, Russia.

☞ **WHEN**   1865.

☞ **WHAT HAS JUST HAPPENED**   The play is based on Russian novelist Dostoyevsky's short story of the same name. This duologue comes at the beginning of the play where Ivan and Zack are at the zoo.

☞ **WHAT TO CONSIDER**

- Despite being set in 1865, the play is written in a very modern style. This lends a deal of humour to the piece and brings its social and political themes bang up to date.

- The difference between the characters. Zack is very much the straight man to Ivan's clown.

- Ivan's inferiority/superiority complex. On the one hand, he is riddled with self-doubt, and on the other, he is consumed with self-importance. Make this integral to your playing of him.

- Zack's envy of Ivan. Notice how easy it is for Zack to declare Ivan a failure as if this justifies his own ordinariness.

- Later on in the play, Anya says of Ivan: 'He's not your friend, Zack, you hate him. You've hated him for years. You only ever wanted him to fail. To embarrass himself and to give up…'

- Both men have had or are in a relationship with Anya. How does this affect their friendship? Read the play to see how this situation develops.

- Both men are in their mid-thirties. It is typically at this time of life that people do settle down but may have to deal with thwarted ambitions and face compromise.

- The scene is quite long. You may prefer to end with Ivan's line: 'They don't want me to be famous, Zack. Because I confront things. Because I'm dangerous. Because I have integrity. You may have heard of it. Even in the legal world…'

☞ **WHAT IVAN WANTS**

- For Zack to understand how hurt he was at being left out.
- To vent his rage at what he considers the stupidities of the world. Think about how this 'venting' helps him to feel better about his own lack of success.
- An audience. Whether he is talking to one person or several hundred, Ivan is the kind of personality that needs to be heard.
- To pursue his ambitions whatever the cost.

☞ **WHAT ZACK WANTS**

- To encourage Ivan to give up trying to be a performer. (Make a decision about what lies behind this. Is he genuinely worried about his friend or does it make Zack's own loss of ambition more palatable?)
- To tell Ivan of his intention to marry Anya. (How important is it for Zack to have Ivan's approval?)

☞ **WHAT THE SCENE IS ABOUT**   Being in one's mid-thirties, the nature of friendship, rivalry, ambition, ego, compromise, refusal to compromise.

☞ **NB**   This play offers a number of other duologues from which to choose.

IVAN. I mean, what is the world coming to!? Genuinely! […] When *this* is the cultural sensation of the age? When this garbage is what passes for entertainment? Some caged cretins napping and pooing! I mean, what are these people doing here? What are they expecting these animals to actually do?

ZACK. They're not expecting anything, Ivan, they've just not seen them before –

IVAN. Oh, this is the end of days! You mark my words. This year will go down in history as the very nadir of human civilisation –

ZACK. You said that last year as well –

IVAN. And we've got worse, haven't we? We've fallen further and fouler! You know why that Darwin bloke worked out we came from these fluffy fucks? You know why that's happening *now*? Because we're turning back in to them, mate. We're devolving. Pretty soon we'll grow fur and tails and beaks and scales and waddle into the sea and turn back into shells.

ZACK. Yup. Did you actually read Darwin's book?

IVAN. I, yes, I read the back.

ZACK. Okay, well, either way, please don't get angry with me about it –

IVAN. I'm not angry with *you*, Zack, I'm angry in general. I'm an artist. That's my job.

ZACK. I, is it – ?

IVAN. I'm angry that the masses lap up this crap! I'm angry about how much it cost to get in here. And, to be honest… I'm still angry that all my friends go out for dinner last night and don't think to invite me!

ZACK. Oh my God, Ivan, please…

IVAN. I mean, how can that happen?!

ZACK. It was an accident –

IVAN. I felt like a goon!

ZACK. I know, I'm sorry –

IVAN. An absolute bloody goon! Plodding past the window with Nikolai Dudin, seeing you, Anne, Pav, Sonya, Andrei polishing off dessert, and Nikolai's like 'Aren't those your friends, Ivan?' and I'm like 'Er… yes, Nikolai, they are – '

ZACK. We couldn't get hold of you –

IVAN. Horseshit!

ZACK. You weren't at home –

IVAN. I'm an actor, Zack, I am always at home!

ZACK. It… okay, look, Ivan… there was a reason you weren't at dinner, that, we… we wanted to –

IVAN. Do you know what I ate last night?

ZACK. Well, no, clearly not –

IVAN. Cheese and turnip.

ZACK. Right, that's… as in?

IVAN. Some cheese and then a turnip. It's not even a meal. It's never even been a meal.

ZACK. Well, okay, you can't pin that on us –

IVAN. I don't like being left out. Ever!

ZACK. It was, yes and I'm saying you weren't left out, per se, it was, we were talking about you, Ivan, about your shows and…

IVAN. Then you bring me here! Rub my face in this shit!

ZACK. I'm not… what? Rubbing your face in what?

IVAN. This is what's stealing my bloody audience, mate! This bilge. These… (*Points at the cockatiel.*) lightweight prats. It's a knife in the nuts bringing me here, it really is…

ZACK. Okay, well I didn't know that, Ivan. I didn't know you were in competition with animals now –

IVAN. I'm in competition with everything, man! And whether I like it or not, and I don't, this is the future of showbiz. Right here. Dancing dogs, weird fish, cross-eyed cats. This'll be the only toss in town before too long, I kid you not. Survival of the bloody blandest. That's what they want…

ZACK. I'm sorry you don't like it here, Ivan, I had no idea that zoos make you angry now as well. We can go and get a coffee once Anya gets here if you'd rather do that.

Beat. IVAN *calms down a bit.*

IVAN. What about my shows? You said you were talking about my shows. At dinner. What about them?

ZACK. Yes. And this is, I don't want to talk about it while you're… het up –

IVAN. I'm not. I've het down now. What were you saying about them?

ZACK. Yeah, okay, look, it wasn't just that we couldn't get hold of you last night, it was more that… we didn't. The truth is, Ivan, we, not just me, Pavel, Anya, a few of us, thought we should talk about you and… your work and, first up, you should know, we all think you're amazingly resilient, how you've kept plugging away all these years despite uh, everything –

IVAN. Uh-huh –

ZACK. But the thing is, we, not just me, felt that it had got to the point where we had to… say something.

IVAN *nods. Beat. A little smile.*

IVAN. You don't…

ZACK. Well… really?

IVAN. I don't do it for praise, Zack.

ZACK. Oh. No, what?

IVAN. I'm just a guy.

ZACK. Yes, I know, sorry, I mean it's not that, it's more the, the other –

IVAN. Say no more…

ZACK. No, I, I think I have to –

IVAN. You'll embarrass me –

ZACK. We think you should stop, Ivan. With the shows. We think it's time you… didn't do them. That was the… what we were talking about.

Long beat.

IVAN. Okay, well, one, no. And two, what?

ZACK. We know you've been finding it tough, money-wise, and –

IVAN. The work is its own reward.

ZACK. Okay. But it's not though, is it?

You're eating cheese and turnip –

IVAN. Yeah, by choice. I like cheese and turnip.

ZACK. Okay. That wasn't the impression you gave me just now –

IVAN. Yes, it was.

ZACK. But, look, that's not the – we think it's maybe… bad for you –

IVAN. The turnip isn't –

ZACK. The work, Ivan. You have to admit, you've become a lot more bitter recently. About people younger than you, people getting more attention than you, about circuses, zoos now, you sound, well… paranoid.

IVAN. Has Anne been saying this?

ZACK. Anya, all of us are worried about you, Ivan, yes. That's all this is.

IVAN. Well… okay, don't. Don't worry –

ZACK. And there comes a point where you have to accept that you gave it a good old go, but it's just not going to happen for you. And that's fine. Giving up is also, sometimes, very brave.

IVAN. Yeah, look, Zack, I know I'm hard-up and tired and, yes, okay, intense, at times. I'm not *buoyant*, like you. I'm complicated. And you're more, not simple but… simpler –

ZACK. Okay, great –

IVAN. We're fundamentally different creatures. Is what I'm saying. I'm a lion, and you're a, you know, a cow. They're both equally good, they're just different –

ZACK. Lions are clearly better –

IVAN. And when you're a lion, as I am, you've got to follow your nature.

You can't just join the herd and grow udders and chew the cud –

ZACK. I don't know what this is meant to mean –

IVAN. It wouldn't work. Everyone'd be like, 'Why is there a lion on the, on your farm?' And the farmer'd be all, 'Is it definitely a lion?' and the, this passer-by figure'd be going, 'Yes, clearly it is, it's roaring and yellow and has talent and things to say – '

ZACK. I think you should abandon this metaphor now, Ivan –

IVAN. I'm not giving up, Zack! I need to perform! Regardless of what's best for me, I just must.

ZACK. Yes, and Anya felt like that at first, but then she started with the cushions and –

IVAN. I have a duty though! To the people –

ZACK. Well… very few people –

IVAN. And to the truth. And to the justice. To expose what's really going on in this country.

ZACK. Yes but, are you confident you actually… know what that is?

IVAN. Very.

ZACK. But I mean… should you be?

IVAN. The arsehole Tsar is selling Russia down the river! I cannot and will not stop until I have brought that tyrant to his bloody knees!

ZACK. I know, Ivan, you've been saying this since college –

IVAN. Yeah, right, because nothing's changed, has it?

ZACK. Well no, of course it has, he's freed the serfs for one thing –

IVAN. Oh, open your eyes, boy! They've not been freed, they've just been released into the free-market feast. Tossed into the jaws of the flesh-eating foreign fat cats. I swear, Zack, when I think about what that man's done to the serfs it makes me physically vomit.

ZACK. But you… why though, Ivan? You don't know any serfs –

IVAN. I know serfs, lad! Don't you worry about that. I've met three of them!

ZACK. You live in the city. And you hang out in cafés, wearing that bloody English hunting jacket!

IVAN. It's a hacking jacket.

ZACK. Moaning about the evil tax-dodging foreign bastards, while blithely buying up their stuff...

IVAN. This was a present from my father –

ZACK. Which you asked for –

IVAN. Which I, this is a very well-made piece of clothes!

ZACK. But you must see the hypocrisy of it, Ivan... you must see that...

Beat.

IVAN. Do you actually believe in me, Zack? In my work?

ZACK. I... if it's not changing anything, if you're not getting anywhere, if the audience for the last one was made up of me, Anya, and that man with the dog, then why... don't keep doing it! Don't keep getting cross with the public because they'd rather watch a bear balancing on a ball than a grown man pretending to be a potato –

IVAN. I wasn't *pretending to be a potato*! Thank you. I was portraying the famine in Northern India from the point of view of the crops – it was highly theatrical. And I'm not cross with the public, I'm cross with the famine. I'm cross it happened –

ZACK. You're cross that you're not famous, Ivan. Be honest. Aren't you?

IVAN. No, I... fame is a curse and I've actively tried to avoid it.

ZACK. Well, congratulations, you've certainly managed that –

IVAN. They don't want me to be famous, Zack. Because I confront things. Because I'm dangerous. Because I have integrity. You may have heard of it. Even in the legal world...

Beat. ZACK turns away frustrated.

And don't describe Mr Poborsky as 'that man with the dog', please –

ZACK. He has got a dog –

IVAN. You're trying to run down my fan! Make him sound like a vagrant –

ZACK. How am I meant to describe him then? I don't know his name –

IVAN. Well… 'the retired headmaster'.

ZACK. I don't know that either –

IVAN. Or maybe 'the distinguished-looking gentleman with the limps'.

ZACK. Okay, fine! I didn't mean to… sorry, *limps*? He's got limps, plural?

IVAN. Yes. One in each leg. Hence why I often delay the start of the show while he's dealing with the stairs.

ZACK. Okay. And do you think that maybe… do you think about that?

IVAN. About what?

ZACK. The fact that, and I don't mean to be blunt, Ivan, that after eight years doing shows, your audience has more limps than paying punters.

IVAN. Do you believe in me, Zack? Cutting to the crap for a sec: do you, my best friend, believe in what I do?

ZACK. I… Ivan, that's not the –

IVAN. Do you actually like it?

Beat.

ZACK. Yes, I…

IVAN *clutches* ZACK*'s shoulder. And smiles at him.*

IVAN. Alright then.

ZACK. The early stuff with Anya, the song-and-dance stuff, was good, but, you know, it's different now, you're not getting any younger –

IVAN. I feel like I am actually… I am full to the brim of beans –

IVAN *starts doing some dance steps.*

ZACK. Everyone's settling down now. Pav and Sonya are having a baby, Andrei's moving out of the city, you're not twenty-five any more, you can't keep doing this, on your own, to a handful of people, slumming it in a tiny flat, into your forties, it's not healthy, Ivan, it's not workable…

IVAN. Mm. They were good, weren't they?

ZACK. What… what's that?

IVAN. The shows with Anne.

ZACK. Oh, yeah, they were great. That wasn't my point though, per se –

IVAN. I've still got the maracas somewhere. Do you think she would – ?

ZACK. No. Ivan.

IVAN. Because you're right, I shouldn't be doing this on my own –

ZACK. Anya makes cushions now –

IVAN. Yeah, I mean, we can fit it in around the cushions, Zack, you can move cushions around, famously –

ZACK. She's moved on.

IVAN. You never really move on –

ZACK. She has, she's –

IVAN *starts busting out a few dance moves. And sings.*

IVAN. 'Don't fear, my dear, the war in the Crimea. We're sending you some cheer and beer and gear from over 'ere…' You're getting married?

IVAN *stops. A bit floored by this.*

ZACK. Yes. I've not actually asked her yet, but, that's, you know, where we're at, where Anya's at. We're settling down. She needs settling. I've been meaning to tell you. To check you were, well not *check*, but just to more, let you know, make sure you were cool with it.

IVAN. Why would I not be cool with it?

ZACK. No, I, exactly, that's why I –

IVAN. I think it's great! This is… yes!

Hugs ZACK.

I am uber-cool with it! This is just good honest… stuff!

ZACK. Thank you. Yeah. Just cos Stefan Maksimushkin
said –

IVAN. Stefan Maksimushkin is full of shit! Whatever it was.
What was it?

ZACK. No, he just, he said you said to him that you thought
one day you and Anya would get back together –

IVAN. That's, no, I didn't say that. And I wouldn't want that.
I would actively hate that in fact –

ZACK. No, good –

IVAN. And not because, don't get me wrong, Anne's lovely,
I just –

ZACK. Well, you don't have to –

IVAN. Annoying. As I'm sure you now know, but that's not,
I'm saying, Stefan Maksimushkin hasn't got any front
teeth.

ZACK. What's that got to do with it?

IVAN. No, nothing, I just also remembered that about him.

ZACK. And he has got front teeth, they're just replacements –

IVAN. They're fake. You shouldn't trust someone who lies
about his teeth.

ZACK. He's not lying, they were knocked out –

IVAN. Sure. All I know is, I'm very pleased, if not relieved
that you're marrying Anne, because a) that's one less thing
for me to worry about –

ZACK. What does that mean?

IVAN. And b) thinking about it, she's been out of the game
for so long now, that getting her gig-fit would take a hell of

a lot of work which frankly I don't have. And time.
I meant.

ZACK. Okay. Great.

IVAN. Have you got the ring?

ZACK finds the ring box in his pocket and passes it to IVAN.

ZACK. Oh yeah, it's... don't say anything, okay? When she
gets here –

IVAN. Yeah, yeah, obviously...

Opens it.

Ahhhhh. Sweet.

ZACK. It's nice isn't it?

IVAN. Lovely. That's... all as I would say, Zack, and feel free
to ignore this, is I don't think it's very 'Anya'. Do you know
what I mean?

He hands it back to him. ZACK stares at him.

ZACK. What are you... why would say that?

IVAN. Just being honest, mate. As per.

God's Property

Arinze Kene

☞ **WHO**   Chima, dual heritage (Irish mother/Nigerian father), late twenties, and Onochie, his brother, mid teens.

☞ **WHERE**   The kitchen of their family's home, Deptford, South London.

☞ **WHEN**   1982. Evening.

☞ **WHAT HAS JUST HAPPENED**   Chima has just been released from prison having served a ten-year sentence for the murder of his white girlfriend, Poppy. For a few days he has been lying low, before arriving back at the family home in Deptford. At the very start of the play, Chima enters through the back door with shopping bags full of food. There is no one in the kitchen. He calls out to his mother and, while he is upstairs looking for her, his younger brother, Onochie, arrives home. Onochie is surprised to find the back door open and the bags on the floor. He assumes that there is a burglar in the house. Then, when Chima comes downstairs, Onochie threatens him with a knife. Onochie has not seen Chima since he was a small boy and in the duologue that follows it takes Chima a while to convince Onochie that he is not an intruder but his older brother.

☞ **WHAT TO CONSIDER**

- The social and political background. Familiarise yourself with the events surrounding the time of the play. Research the Brixton riots, the New Cross fire and 'Operation Swamp'.

- The difficulties growing up mixed-race in a largely white and racist environment in 1982.

- The risk Chima is taking by returning home. Graham, Sylvia and Liam (Poppy's father, mother and brother), live across the road. As soon as they spot Chima, they will be out for revenge.

- Chima's shock at seeing Onochie dressed as a 'skinhead'.

- Onochie prefers to identify himself as white. Chima, on the other hand, has learned that in the eyes of the world, he will only ever be regarded as black.

- While in prison, Chima has come to identify with the struggles of his black 'brothers', many of whom are unemployed, and who have been rioting in Brixton, some even dying in police custody.

- Read the play to discover how Poppy was in fact killed by her own father, and how it was decided that, in order to protect Onochie, Chima should take the blame.

- Make a decision about how Chima's innocence of the murder and continued pretence to the contrary has affected him.

- Although at this point in the play Onochie is unaware of the fact, their mother has committed suicide. Chima has found a suicide note, which he tears up shortly after this scene.

- Think about how Chima is carrying this 'secret' throughout the duologue. To what extent does he blame himself? Why does he not tell Onochie?

- The struggles experienced by their Nigerian father, who eventually died of alcoholism, following dismissal from the Post Office for having a nose bleed. 'They didn't like that he bled everywhere.'

- The knives. There are strict rules about using real knives in the rehearsal room and on stage. You will most probably need to work with plastic/pretend blades unless you are under the supervision of a trained and professional fight director.

- The scene is quite long. You may prefer to end with Chima's line: 'You want it to be my fault.'

☞ WHAT ONOCHIE WANTS

- To distance himself from Chima (both personally and politically).

- To safeguard his home from attack.

- To protect his mother.

- To demonstrate his manhood.

☞ WHAT CHIMA WANTS

- Refuge.
- To protect Onochie from the truth about why their mother is missing.
- To create a sense of family. (Notice how he wants to cook the kind of food from his childhood.)

☞ **WHAT THE SCENE IS ABOUT** The need to belong and to feel safe, to move on from the past and to readjust, suspicion, loyalty, trust.

☞ **NB** This play offers a number of other duologues from which to choose.

ONOCHIE […] *pulls out a flick knife. He flicks it open and nervously holds it out just as* CHIMA *enters the kitchen. Beat.* CHIMA *and* ONOCHIE *lock eyes with each other, both frozen.* […]

CHIMA. Ay.

ONOCHIE. Ay.

CHIMA. Ay.

ONOCHIE. Come on then!

CHIMA. Look.

ONOCHIE. Move!

CHIMA. I.

ONOCHIE. Move…

CHIMA. Listen –

ONOCHIE. Move back.

CHIMA. I'm…

ONOCHIE. Step back.

CHIMA. Stepping…

ONOCHIE. Back.

CHIMA. Stepping back look.

ONOCHIE. I'll…

CHIMA. Please –

ONOCHIE. I'll do it yer.

CHIMA. Put –

ONOCHIE. Explain.

CHIMA. Put that –

ONOCHIE. What the fuck –

CHIMA. Put it down.

ONOCHIE. Explain what the fuck –

CHIMA. Am I doing here?

ONOCHIE. Upstair!

CHIMA. I was looking –

ONOCHIE. Yer shouldn't 'ave been.

CHIMA. No, listen, I was looking for –

ONOCHIE. Yer nicking stuff – (*Kicks* CHIMA's *bag.*)

CHIMA. Nah, this is my –

ONOCHIE. Yer what?

CHIMA. House.

ONOCHIE. Yer…

CHIMA. House.

ONOCHIE. Not possible.

CHIMA. Yeah.

ONOCHIE. Well, that's…

CHIMA. The truth.

ONOCHIE. The wrong answer, mate.

CHIMA. 14 Eddon Street.

ONOCHIE. Where *I* live.

CHIMA. Me too.

ONOCHIE. Yer…

CHIMA. Yes.

ONOCHIE. Yer obviously…

CHIMA. Got a bedroom upstairs.

ONOCHIE. Yer obviously wanna catch a stabbing.

CHIMA. Ono, listen.

ONOCHIE. WHAT?

CHIMA. Onochie.

ONOCHIE. Who the fuck…

CHIMA. See –

ONOCHIE. Who are yer?

CHIMA. I know your name cos –

ONOCHIE. HOW?

CHIMA. It's me.

ONOCHIE. Don't…

CHIMA. Please –

ONOCHIE. If yer move –

CHIMA. But you're –

ONOCHIE. Stop mo–

CHIMA. You got a knife at me.

ONOCHIE. Stop shuffling around then.

CHIMA. Okay!

ONOCHIE. OKAY!

CHIMA. Just. Now. Just.

ONOCHIE. Stab.

CHIMA. No need.

ONOCHIE. I will.

CHIMA. There is no need for that.

ONOCHIE (*suddenly panicking*). Fuck! Fuck.

Where's –

CHIMA. Calm down.

ONOCHIE. She.

  She were 'ere before I left.

CHIMA. That's. That's what I'm trying to –

ONOCHIE. Where is…

CHIMA. It's why I was upstairs…

ONOCHIE. She's upstair –

CHIMA. I don't think she's here…

ONOCHIE. Where did she go?

CHIMA. Well, I just got in so I didn't catch her leaving –

ONOCHIE. She fuckin' here or not!

CHIMA. She ain't here I said –

ONOCHIE. Wait-wait-wait did yer…

CHIMA. No.

ONOCHIE. Yer 'urt 'er?

CHIMA. Course I never!

ONOCHIE. Yer went up and did what to 'er – I'll kill yer –

CHIMA. She's… behind you, look.

> ONOCHIE *looks over his shoulder and in that moment*
> CHIMA *skilfully disarms him and now has the knife*
> (CHIMA *could have him if he wanted to*). *Beat, as*
> ONOCHIE *looks at* CHIMA *then back at his own empty*
> *hand.*

ONOCHIE. Thass not funny.

CHIMA. Nah.

ONOCHIE. Give it here.

CHIMA. Ono, please –

ONOCHIE. Suit yerself.

> ONOCHIE *grabs a kitchen knife out of a drawer – they're*
> *now both holding up knives, walking around.* ONOCHIE
> *comes lunging at* CHIMA *more aggressively now.*

CHIMA. OI!

ONOCHIE. Yer think I won't do yer –

CHIMA. Let's stop this.

ONOCHIE. THEN TELL ME WHERE SHE IS!

CHIMA. It's me. Chim.

ONOCHIE. Jim?

CHIMA. Chima.

ONOCHIE. Chima?!

CHIMA. Yes.

ONOCHIE. No, 'e's, uh…

CHIMA. It's me, Ono.

ONOCHIE. Do I look like some –

CHIMA. It's me.

ONOCHIE. Some prick.

CHIMA. Chima.

ONOCHIE. Nah.

CHIMA. Your brother.

ONOCHIE. Ma brother, is it?

CHIMA. Yes.

ONOCHIE. Yer juss…

CHIMA. Yes.

ONOCHIE. Yer juss beggin' to get stab now.

CHIMA. Nah.

ONOCHIE. 'Oo else…

CHIMA. Just me.

ONOCHIE. …In my 'ouse.

CHIMA. I'm alone.

ONOCHIE. Fuckin'…

CHIMA. Chima.

ONOCHIE. Yer ain't…

CHIMA. Bro, listen –

ONOCHIE. Yer ain't 'im!

CHIMA. Look, I can prove –

ONOCHIE. TAKE –

CHIMA. Sorry.

ONOCHIE. YER 'ANDS OUT YER POCKETS!

CHIMA *slams his knife down on to the table.*

CHIMA. Fuck's sake, man, upstairs… the first door… that's my bedroom, yours is the second door, Mum's Irish, Dad's black, Nigerian, Dad was a – you were six years old, when he died, we uh, we used to go church when he was here, and uh you me and him would cook together, every Sunday, that was our thing. Onochie Chukwu Igwe is your full name, all down your leg you got a birthmark, goes all the way down, Mum says… she used to say it's cos she had an itchy leg when she was carrying you – Mum… Mum, don't like touching cardboard, said she hates the texture… she'd sing to us this made-up breakfast song when she cooked in the mornings: '*Eggy deggy*…' – we'd sit, around this table, the four of us… this is where Dad sat, you always were sat there, Mum would be the last to sit down every time as she'd have dished it all so she'd sit there, and that was my place…

I'm your brother.

It's me.

ONOCHIE *stares at him – still holding the knife up.*

(*Re: knife.*) Come on.

A moment, and then ONOCHIE *lets his arm come down. Shakes his head. Puts the kitchen knife away and takes his own off the table – he paces.*

ONOCHIE. 'Ow comes yer 'ere?

CHIMA. –

ONOCHIE. What yer 'ere for?

CHIMA *sits in his chair.*

Beat.

CHIMA. Sit down here with me for a sec.

ONOCHIE. Mum! Mum!

CHIMA. She ain't here –

ONOCHIE. Yer made her leave.

CHIMA. I didn't make her do anything.

ONOCHIE. Yeah yer did. Yer did cos she'd normally be 'ome this time.

CHIMA. Bro. Sit down.

ONOCHIE. She knew you were coming, didn't she? Cos that were you last week. Yer phoned up. Fuckin' knew it – that were you, weren't it? What'd yer say to 'er? Had 'er crying in the toilet afterwards. What 'ave yer done?

CHIMA. She was –

ONOCHIE. Leakin'. Cos of summit yer said.

CHIMA. Told her I'd be passing, that's all.

ONOCHIE (*pointed*). Well, that'll do it. To push her out the door, thass more than enough!

CHIMA. Ono, sit down a moment.

ONOCHIE. I'll sit down when yer fucked off, yer prick. Yer ain't welcome. She'd a' been upset with yer bein' 'ere! Yer made 'er walk out!

CHIMA. You're gonna change your tone of voice.

ONOCHIE. Do not threaten me!

You.

Do not.

Threaten.

Me!

Ain't 'fraid of yer.

CHIMA. Respect. Don't need you to 'fraid me just respect that I'm older –

ONOCHIE. Yer oughta know respect goes both ways – gimme that / older-brother shit…

CHIMA. You're foaming at the mouth – I've done nothing to you.

ONOCHIE. Yer in me 'ouse for one, / uninvited…

CHIMA. My house as much as it is yours.

ONOCHIE. Scared me mum off, she's already in a fragile state, now thanks to you, she could be out there crying, walking up an' down some bridge –

CHIMA. Don't say that –

ONOCHIE. Again! It's true. Yer ain' done enough already, yer wanna come back and finish 'er off. Fuck's sake.

CHIMA. –

ONOCHIE. Now, is that all what's 'appened?

CHIMA. Is what all what's happen–

ONOCHIE. What yer tellin' me, son, what yer just said.

That yer came and now she's gone.

Beat.

Yer even listening?! (*Checks* CHIMA's *eyes.*) Hiding something. Yep. Fuckin' know it.

CHIMA *looks away.* ONOCHIE *reads this as him hiding something.*

(*Points his finger close to* CHIMA's *face.*) Look, more deceit.

CHIMA. You wanna get out of my face and calm down.

ONOCHIE *paces and boots* CHIMA's *bag.*

What did I just say?

ONOCHIE. It's what yer *not* saying!

ONOCHIE *boots* CHIMA's *bag again.*

CHIMA (*standing*). Do that again and see if I don't cancel your birth.

Beat.

ONOCHIE *looks at the bag. He walks to it and boots it again.* CHIMA *stares at* ONOCHIE – *he'd like to rip his head off but he sits back down at the table.*

You want it to be my fault.

ONOCHIE. Whose fault is it? Let's 'ave a twig at the math: yer show up outta nowhere, my mum suddenly up and leaves – you equal trouble.

CHIMA. That's what you reckon.

ONOCHIE. Thass what I know.

CHIMA. Well then, you don't know much, a lot, or a little bit.

ONOCHIE. I do know what's in yer nature. And obviously yer made 'er feel so uncomfortable in 'er own 'ome that she's 'ad to leave.

CHIMA. –

ONOCHIE. She don't want yer 'ere, man. Spelled it out to me a fuckin' trillion times, she don't like yer. Yer a disgrace, she says. 'Cording to her she only got the one son.

CHIMA. Yeah.

ONOCHIE. She's buried yer. Yer don't exist any more.

CHIMA. Did Mum *say* that – yes or no?

ONOCHIE. Says it all the time! Being honest 'ere, she's too nice to show yer forthright what she's truly thinking. *I* personally feel no way in relaying this to yer on the other 'and: she don't want yer 'ere. Say the neighbours see yer, then what? Yer thought 'bout that? They're only 'cross the road, for fuck's sake – yer fan club. Yer don't think, man. About what could happen. Yer comin' back 'ere, seriously, yer not right in yer 'ead.

CHIMA. You're my little brother. I wanted to see you, so I'm here, / what's wrong about that?

ONOCHIE. Why the hellfuck yer wanna see *me*, I don't know.

CHIMA. Haven't had connection with you in ten years – I'm not even complaining that you lot didn't come to visit me, not once. Know how that felt?! Other people, worst things they done, their families at least showed up for them once a year – wrote them, whatever.

ONOCHIE. Yer a grown man so I'll admit, setting down to write yer birthday cards dint cross me mind.

Lissen, we've nothin' in common but a surname. Other than that, what makes me connected to yer? Nothing.

CHIMA. –

ONOCHIE. Us to pretend everything's hunky-dory like yer dint do as yer done. We don't need yer sashaying through Deptford dressed in yer long humiliations, thank yer very much.

There's no way better sayin' this, no one wants yer round 'ere. No one. Yer only know deep down what it's gonna do to Mum – Is that it – that's yer intention? Cos yer going the right way about it.

Long beat.

CHIMA. She told me to look after you.

ONOCHIE. Mate. Do I… do I look like a pillock – yer just said she weren't 'ere when yer came.

CHIMA. When I phoned, when I told her I was coming, she said okay, she told me to look after you and yeah that's pillock's uniform you got on.

ONOCHIE. Why would she tell yer to look after me?

CHIMA. Said she wanted us to talk. And… thinking about it, maybe that's why she's not here. To give us some time alone. Catch up on each other. Make sense of all this.

Pause. ONOCHIE *shakes his head at this – he realises something.*

ONOCHIE. Fuck.

ONOCHIE *sits – something weighs heavy on his mind.*

CHIMA. We're brothers, Ono.

ONOCHIE. That is not relevant. She… she said all that to yer?

CHIMA. I wouldn't lie to you.

ONOCHIE. –

CHIMA. What.

ONOCHIE. Oh, it's nothing really, only that she's not said a word since last week. Since yer phoned that afternoon. Morning till night she's in bed. Won't say a word.

CHIMA. –

ONOCHIE. So let's, let's just backtrack, for a moment, rig the conversation that yer had with her, objectively: a depressive mother says to yer 'I need yer to look after my son.' And that don't sound odd to yer? No flag raised. It sounds normal to yer. It didn't sound at all a bit 'thank you goodnight'.

CHIMA. Didn't sound odd at the time.

ONOCHIE. How's it sounding now?

You've done this, ya know.

CHIMA. Mum's had issues.

ONOCHIE. 'Mum's had issues'? Yer gonna stand there and say Mum had issues?

CHIMA. She did –

ONOCHIE. She had issues because she had you! Yer the fuckin' issues, Chima! Really… yer summit else. Yer summit else altogether.

Left Mum to do all the cleanin' up of yer shit and yer have the guts to imply she's brought it on 'erself? She's gone through hell cos of yer. We've 'ad to take it from all the lot 'round 'ere. Been humiliated. It's all died down now thanks to me but we can't 'ave yer bring the trouble back to this 'ouse – This ain' a prodigal-son thing where yer return 'ome an' we give yer some big celebration, huge feast with an assortment of meats an' fish, nah. Yer must've 'ad yer legs crossed when yer made that wish. So excuse me if I don't leap at the opportunity to 'bond' with yer. The damage is irreparable, son. Yer can't spit back the chunk of flesh that yer tore out of this family.

ONOCHIE *goes to the door and opens it wide –*

I say yer'll 'ave to leave.

Grab yer shit, sling yer hook, yer gonna 'ave to get off. Let the door 'it yer where the dog shoulda bit yer.

CHIMA. You know what's out there for me.

ONOCHIE. Not my problem. Yer just come from out there to get 'ere so yer taken the risk already.

CHIMA. You don't care what happens to me.

ONOCHIE. Son, I'll tell yer what I do care about – I care about me mum. I care about strangers, in me 'ome, upsetting me mum. Man of the 'ouse? Me. Gotta protect 'er. So let's go, I can't leave yer in 'ere alone case she comes back and finds yer poncin'.

CHIMA *doesn't move.*

Look. Yer know that yer ain't entitled to be 'ere. She'll die of shame. Tell yer what, when I find 'er, I'll tell 'er yer said yer never meant to scare 'er off. What's more, Chim, I'll tell 'er that yer said yer sorry. Which is what yer never did say, Chim. Not to me, not to my mum… poor Sylvia, Old Graham and Liam across the way, they ain't had a sorry out of yer. Never showed any remorse. Up till now. But I'll tell 'er that yer did. How's that?

Beat. CHIMA *nods. He starts to go to his bag on the floor –*

Good, man.

But CHIMA *begins bringing groceries and other foods out of the bag and putting them on the table. He looks to* ONOCHIE.

CHIMA. You're angry. I haven't been here for you and Mum. Okay. I'm here now. I walked all the way here. I've had to make my bed in a stairwell the last couple nights. I have not been smiling these past ten years. I haven't had pleasure from all this badness and discord. I ask that you please just for one moment think back to when we were okay. My best memory of us as a family is when you, Dad and me would cook on Sundays. Proper Nigerian food. You used to love that. If you can give me that, and let me clean myself up good and proper, rest my head on my pillow for a while… I'd be grateful. That's all I ask. What I am saying is that there are two types of pain you can feel here, little brother. The pain of putting up with me, for a little while. Or the pain of regret, that is everlasting. That you wear under your skin. Speaking from experience.

Silence.

ONOCHIE. The time is 18:50.

Yer sleep, shit, shower, shave, eat, drink, whatever. I'll give yer till dark, as it'll be less heated for yer walking through Deptford at that time. Yer get to stay 'ere until and not a minute after midnight. After that, yer gone – yer leave, yer don't come back. Thass me being generous. I won't be participating in any cooking of Nigerian food with yer this evening and nor will I be eating it. Yer just do yer thing and I'll do mine.

Agree to that.

Beat.

CHIMA *nods.*

Once it hits twelve yer gotta be out 'ere like yer chariot's gonna pumpkin.

CHIMA *nods.*

Not a minute after.

CHIMA. Okay.

ONOCHIE. Yer see, I want for it to be crystal clear that I ain' bein' tough for nothin' –

CHIMA. I said okay.

ONOCHIE. No, lissen, lissen, Mum wouldn't want yer 'ere is all –

I 'ave to protect 'er.

Is what I 'ave to do.

CHIMA. You're doing a good job –

ONOCHIE. If I don't – yeah, I know I am – if I don't, no one else will.

CHIMA. Not arguing with you, you're right.

ONOCHIE. Yer fuckin' right, I'm right.

The Initiate

Alexandra Wood

☞ **WHO**   Man, a Somali taxi driver living in London, and Younger Man, a Somali pirate.

☞ **WHERE**   Somalia.

☞ **WHEN**   Present day.

☞ **WHAT HAS JUST HAPPENED**   The Man, whose name is Dalmar, is a London taxi driver. He loves his job and the city in which he works. So much so, that he has been taking his passengers on detours in order to show them the sights. But when a number of women complain about how unsafe they feel in his cab, Dalmar loses his job. Dalmar is from Somalia, and it is obvious to him that these women were unable to distinguish his good intentions from the murderous acts of Somali pirates. Dalmar is affronted by this, so – when a local British couple are captured on holiday, and his son is bullied at school because he looks like a picture of one of the pirates – he takes it upon himself to secure their release. In the duologue that follows he has travelled to Somalia and has met with one of the men holding the British couple captive.

☞ **WHAT TO CONSIDER**

- The story bears a close resemblance to the real-life case of the Chandlers, who were held captive for over a year and released after a ransom was paid.

- The inherent racism that Somalis experience living in the UK. (Interestingly, as I was writing this commentary, the word 'pirates' automatically showed in the suggestions bar after I had typed in 'Somali' in a search engine.)

- Dalmar has lived in Britain for twenty years. His sons were born there, and he considers himself British.

- The portrayal of the Younger Man. We know that what he does is wrong and appalling, but he is also human and therefore has characteristics that we warm to. It is important that you capture both his charm and brutality.

- The humour. Despite the play's violent background and serious subject matter, the duologue is also funny.

- The play is intended for three actors. In the playscript the characters are described generically as Man, Younger Man and Woman. Between them they play ten parts.

- By identifying the characters in this way, to what extent does the play suggest that there is essentially very little difference between people?

- Read the play to find out whether the Younger Man succeeds in corrupting the Man.

- The scene is quite long. You may prefer to end with the Man's line: 'I don't. I don't want anything from you.'

☞ WHAT THE MAN WANTS

- To succeed in his negotiations.

- To challenge the morality of the Younger Man.

- To distance himself from the Younger Man. (He loathes the fact that he has been tarred with the same brush: 'How will we ever get anywhere if people like you continue to do whatever you want.')

☞ WHAT THE YOUNGER MAN WANTS

- More money.

- To get the Man onside. If he can corrupt him, this will mean in turn more money.

- Status.

- Respect. (Notice how he hates to be the underdog: 'I know what it's like when people take advantage of you.')

- To practise and improve his English.

☞ WHAT THE SCENE IS ABOUT   Identity, belonging, altruism, greed, survival.

☞ NB   This play offers a number of other duologues from which to choose.

YOUNGER MAN. I'd rather speak in English.

MAN. Not on my account.

YOUNGER MAN. No. I need the practice. And as a guy who's lived there, you'll know all the slang. I like slang.

MAN. My sons would probably be better for that kind of thing.

YOUNGER MAN. Are they here?

MAN. No.

YOUNGER MAN. Then you'll do.

Pause.

I've been trying to speak to the couple / but they're

MAN. How are they?

YOUNGER MAN. Okay. Why would they not be?

MAN. You're holding them hostage.

YOUNGER MAN. I'm not a thug.

What's another word for that?

MAN. Are they coping?

YOUNGER MAN. What's another word for that? I want to expand my vocabulary.

MAN. Why?

YOUNGER MAN. To get better of course. How else would you say it, thug?

MAN. I don't know.

YOUNGER MAN. You've come here for my help haven't you? You can give me a few words. What do the newspapers in Britain call us?

MAN. I don't know.

YOUNGER MAN. You won't offend me.

MAN. Pirates.

YOUNGER MAN. Is that all?

MAN. You're not in the news for long.

The Government won't give you the money.

YOUNGER MAN. There was an Australian man on a cargo ship we captured and he called us crooks. I like that word. We let him go. After they gave us two million dollars, but also because he gave me a new word. Crook.

MAN. Your English is better than mine.

YOUNGER MAN. Thank you. Do they use this word in Britain or is it just in Australia?

MAN. No, we use it too.

YOUNGER MAN. We?

MAN. I didn't realise this was going to be an English lesson.

YOUNGER MAN. You've travelled all the way here, you might as well share what you have.

Pause.

MAN. Are you planning on coming to the UK?

YOUNGER MAN. Would they want me? A crook.

MAN. Is that what you want the money for? To get out of here.

YOUNGER MAN. Do I ask you why you have a job?

MAN. What you do isn't a job.

YOUNGER MAN. Oh, what is the right word for it?

Business?

You have come here to do business with me.

MAN. I've come here to negotiate with you.

YOUNGER MAN. Are they different?

MAN. I'm not an expert.

YOUNGER MAN. In language or in business?

MAN. Neither of them.

YOUNGER MAN. So why did they send you?

MAN. No one sent me here.

YOUNGER MAN. Then why did you come?

MAN. To help.

YOUNGER MAN. You can help by giving me the money we've asked for.

MAN. I can't do that.

YOUNGER MAN. Then you can't help.

MAN. I can give you some money.

YOUNGER MAN. How much?

MAN. A quarter of a million.

YOUNGER MAN. What is another word for idiot?

MAN. Stupid.

YOUNGER MAN. I know that word. Another word.

MAN. Fool.

YOUNGER MAN. I know that word. Another word.

MAN. I don't know.

YOUNGER MAN. Do you think I'm a moron?

MAN. No.

YOUNGER MAN. My Australian friend taught me moron.

MAN. He's not a friend if you capture him and hold him hostage.

YOUNGER MAN. I let him live. That was friendly wasn't it?

Pause.

MAN. I don't think you're a moron.

YOUNGER MAN. Good. Then maybe we can be friends.

MAN. No one sent me here. I went to the Somali community in the UK and I asked them to donate as much as they could. Which they did. I paid for a ticket and here I am. To negotiate.

YOUNGER MAN. There's nothing to negotiate if you only have two hundred and fifty thousand pounds.

MAN. It's better than nothing.

YOUNGER MAN. We want five million. A quarter of a million is an insult.

MAN. We don't have that much.

Pause.

YOUNGER MAN. What is your job?

MAN. I drive a cab.

YOUNGER MAN. You went all the way to London to drive a car?

What car do you drive?

MAN. A Ford Mondeo.

YOUNGER MAN. You went all the way to London to drive a Ford Mondeo?

No surprise you have come back.

MAN. It's a good job.

YOUNGER MAN. Maybe if you have a good car.

MAN. It's a good job.

YOUNGER MAN. Who do you drive?

MAN. People.

YOUNGER MAN. Government officials?

MAN. Businessmen. People like that.

YOUNGER MAN. People like me.

MAN. No.

YOUNGER MAN. If I came to London would you drive me around?

MAN. If you came to London and tried to do what you do here you'd never get away with it. It's a different kind of place.

YOUNGER MAN. London has no crooks?

MAN. If you came to London and demanded five million pounds for kidnapping someone they'd laugh at you.

YOUNGER MAN. Of course. I'd demand at least ten million if I was in London.

MAN. They'd track you down and put you away.

YOUNGER MAN. But I'm not in London.

And neither are you.

Pause.

MAN. I can think of lots of things I'd do with a quarter of a million pounds.

YOUNGER MAN. What?

MAN. Buy a house.

YOUNGER MAN. That's one thing.

MAN. A big thing.

YOUNGER MAN. Nearly fifty of us need to be paid. And we all have families who expect something.

MAN. The longer the negotiations go on the more everyone will expect.

YOUNGER MAN. I'm telling you if a quarter of a million is all you have then go right now.

Pause.

So you have more.

MAN. I can go a little higher, but not much.

YOUNGER MAN. How much is a little?

MAN. A hundred thousand.

YOUNGER MAN. Very little.

MAN. It's a lot here.

YOUNGER MAN. For people like us?

MAN. It goes further here than in other places.

YOUNGER MAN. How long have you been back?

MAN. Long enough to know the price of things.

YOUNGER MAN. And how long have you been away?

Pause.

How long have you been away?

MAN. I send money to my family, I know how much things cost.

YOUNGER MAN. I give money to my family too. I can't do that with four hundred thousand.

MAN. I said three hundred and fifty.

YOUNGER MAN. I can do even less with that.

Pause.

These people have a yacht. Their family can pay.

MAN. Their family have contributed but they're not millionaires.

YOUNGER MAN. Would they give their money to you?

MAN. It's not for me, it's for you.

YOUNGER MAN. But would they trust you with it?

You look like me.

MAN. No I don't.

YOUNGER MAN. You're fatter. But to them, you look like me.

MAN. I'm not like you.

YOUNGER MAN. You look like me.

MAN. I went to them personally and I told them I wanted to bring their parents back.

YOUNGER MAN. What was their house like?

MAN. Normal.

YOUNGER MAN. Do they own it?

MAN. I didn't ask.

YOUNGER MAN. Why not?

MAN. Because it's rude.

YOUNGER MAN. You are coming here, to negotiate with pirates, with crooks, to save their parents. I think you can ask.

MAN. They were very upset. They gave what they have.

Pause.

YOUNGER MAN. You work for the Government?

MAN. No.

YOUNGER MAN. You drive a Ford Mondeo?

MAN. Yes.

YOUNGER MAN. I wouldn't give you my money.

MAN. Well they did. Which is what I'm offering you now.

YOUNGER MAN. How much do you have?

MAN. I've told you.

YOUNGER MAN. No. At first you had two hundred and fifty. After a few minutes you had three hundred and fifty. How much will you have in an hour?

MAN. If I worked for the Government I'd be better at this wouldn't I?

YOUNGER MAN. You could be pretending to be an idiot.

Pause.

MAN. These people were just on holiday. They weren't fishing in your waters. They weren't dumping toxic waste in your waters. They aren't a threat to you.

YOUNGER MAN. No.

MAN. So how can you justify holding them hostage?

YOUNGER MAN. They're British.

MAN. So am I.

YOUNGER MAN. Perhaps I should hold you hostage as well.

Pause.

Relax. I wouldn't do that.

If this is all I get for them, what would I get for you?

Silence.

Don't be upset. It's just business.

You're thinking, why did I come here?

So am I. If you only came with three hundred and fifty thousand.

MAN. I'm your only chance to make some money out of this.

YOUNGER MAN. I think so too.

That's why I'm not interested in peanuts.

The Australian taught me that. I like it.

MAN. Three hundred and fifty thousand pounds isn't peanuts.

YOUNGER MAN. It means a small amount, doesn't it?

MAN. That's not a small amount.

YOUNGER MAN. Divided by fifty it is. I want walnuts.

MAN. You can't say that.

YOUNGER MAN. You know what I mean don't you?

Pause.

What slang would your sons teach me?

MAN. I don't know.

YOUNGER MAN. Words they don't use with you.

MAN. I don't know.

YOUNGER MAN. Words they use with their friends.

Do they have many friends?

Pause.

MAN. Five million is unreasonable.

YOUNGER MAN. Is it? For two lives?

MAN. You must expect to compromise.

YOUNGER MAN. I don't like that word.

MAN. You say you're not a thug.

What do you imagine people think of you?

YOUNGER MAN. People don't think of me.

Do you imagine they think of you?

If you save this pair they might.

They might call you a hero.

They might invite you to Buckingham Palace for afternoon tea.

I think you need to offer more than three hundred and fifty for that.

MAN. It's all I have.

YOUNGER MAN. I don't believe you.

How many times have you driven past Buckingham Palace in your Ford Mondeo? I bet you'd like to go in.

MAN. Do you imagine you're helping Somalia?

YOUNGER MAN. I don't spend much time imagining.

MAN. How will we ever get anywhere if people like you continue to do whatever you want?

YOUNGER MAN. I don't want to get anywhere. I am somewhere. I'm here.

MAN. And what kind of life can you have here?

YOUNGER MAN. Do you imagine you're helping Somalia by leaving?

You're helping yourself. Not Somalia. Just like you're helping yourself by coming back.

MAN. I could help you too, but you won't let me.

YOUNGER MAN. Three hundred and / fifty isn't

MAN. What's the least you'll accept?

YOUNGER MAN. Do you think I'm a moron?

MAN. Do you think I am?

YOUNGER MAN. Yes.

MAN. Well I'm not. I will walk away and you will have nothing. Don't think I won't walk away. You should be careful.

YOUNGER MAN. You're threatening a pirate?

I could kill you as well as the couple.

MAN. Then you would definitely be a thug.

YOUNGER MAN. A businessman.

If I kill you and them, next time, I will definitely get the money I ask for.

MAN. Or prison.

You accepted two million before. With the cargo ship. This is a small sailing boat. You only have two hostages. You can't expect to get five million.

YOUNGER MAN. Inflation.

MAN. That was less than a year ago.

Pause.

Is there someone else I can speak to?

YOUNGER MAN. Why? Don't you like me?

MAN. You think I'm a moron. You won't negotiate with me. Fine. Is there someone who will?

YOUNGER MAN. You take it personally?

MAN. I'm not an idiot. Do you think it's easy to leave? Do you think it's easy, it isn't easy, and that's why you haven't done it.

YOUNGER MAN. Do you want a medal?

MAN. I don't want anything from you.

YOUNGER MAN. That's not true.

Pause.

MAN. I don't.

I don't want anything from you.

YOUNGER MAN. I can't accept less than three million.

Pause.

Do not smile.

MAN. At first you wanted five million. After ten minutes you'll take three. How much will you accept in an hour?

Pause.

YOUNGER MAN. You don't want to go back without the couple. What would you say to the people who gave you money? What would you say to your sons?

MAN. I tried. That's more than anyone else.

YOUNGER MAN. But you don't want to say that.

Do you get invited to Buckingham Palace for trying?

MAN. I don't know what you have to do.

YOUNGER MAN. Do you have three million?

MAN. No.

YOUNGER MAN. Then why are you smiling?

Pause.

Do you negotiate your cab fares?

MAN. No.

YOUNGER MAN. Why not?

MAN. There are fixed prices.

YOUNGER MAN. So you thought you'd practise with a pirate instead?

MAN. This isn't practice, I don't want a career in this. I don't want to do this again. I'm only doing it to help the Clarkes get home.

YOUNGER MAN. If that's all you want why didn't you pay a professional?

MAN. I don't need a professional qualification to come here and speak to my people.

YOUNGER MAN. You said you are British.

MAN. And you said I look the same as you.

Can we speak in Somali?

YOUNGER MAN. Why?

MAN. It's our language.

YOUNGER MAN. I've told you, I want to learn English slang. But you don't know much.

MAN. I want to speak our language.

YOUNGER MAN. I speak it all the time.

The couple don't know much either.

Too old I suppose.

Pause.

MAN. Can I see them?

YOUNGER MAN. You think they're dead?

MAN. I'd like to see them. So they know they're not alone.

YOUNGER MAN. There are always guards with them. They know they're not alone.

MAN. I mean, so they know we're trying to help them.

YOUNGER MAN. You think they want to see your face?

Your face is like my face.

How will they know you're not one of us?

MAN. Their children wanted me to pass on a message.

YOUNGER MAN. Why didn't their children come here themselves?

MAN. Because it's

Because I came.

YOUNGER MAN. They let you come because it doesn't matter if we kill you.

MAN. They trusted me to come for them.

YOUNGER MAN. They let you come because they're scared.

MAN. Yes they're scared.

Their parents are being held by pirates. Of course they're scared.

Their parents are in some crazy African country that is only ever in the news for pirates or war or death.

They are terrified.

I didn't need to ask them if they own their house. I know they've given me everything they have.

YOUNGER MAN. What is the message?

MAN. It's for their parents.

YOUNGER MAN. What is the message?

MAN. I'm sure you can guess what it is.

YOUNGER MAN. Tell me.

MAN. What do you think it might be?

YOUNGER MAN. Tell me.

MAN. Let me tell them.

YOUNGER MAN. You ask for a lot and don't give me anything.

MAN. I've offered three hundred and fifty thousand pounds. Cash. Not a pie in the sky, but real cash.

YOUNGER MAN. Pie in the sky?

MAN. Three million is a pie in the sky.

YOUNGER MAN. Is that slang?

MAN. It means it's a dream. Not going to happen. And you know it.

YOUNGER MAN. I like it. Pie in the sky.

Pause.

Were they crying? Their children.

MAN. No.

YOUNGER MAN. Their grandchildren?

MAN. I didn't meet them.

YOUNGER MAN. Why not?

MAN. They're very young. They don't understand what's happening.

YOUNGER MAN. They kept them from you.

MAN. Why would they do that?

YOUNGER MAN. You should be an honoured guest. They should line up to kiss your feet. But you're just a messenger.

MAN. They're terrified. I don't expect them to wait on me.

YOUNGER MAN. But when you get back?

Pause.

I know what it's like when people take advantage of you.

MAN. They're not taking advantage of me. I offered to come here.

YOUNGER MAN. And they let you.

I know what it's like.

But I'm standing up for myself now.

MAN. Is that what this is?

The Clarkes weren't taking advantage of you.

YOUNGER MAN. But they're taking advantage of you.

Don't let them.

Don't let them take advantage of either of us. I can't accept three hundred and fifty.

Let's work together.

It's what they expect.

You could buy a house. I could build a house.

Brother.

They sent you out here to die.

MAN. No.

YOUNGER MAN. You told me. All they know of Somalia is pirates and death. So what do they think will happen to you?

They expect you to die. Or to cheat them. Which would you prefer?

If we are organised, this could be a successful business.

MAN. Why did they give me their money?

YOUNGER MAN. Some money. An amount they can lose. A gamble.

MAN. It's more than that.

YOUNGER MAN. How much?

Pause.

They have a yacht.

MAN. That's all they have.

They believe you would kill them. Why would they gamble with their parents' lives?

YOUNGER MAN. You don't know them.

Maybe they don't like their parents.

MAN. They're close.

YOUNGER MAN. Then why are they sailing the seas?

MAN. For adventure.

YOUNGER MAN. Maybe to get away from their family.

Is that why you left?

MAN. No.

YOUNGER MAN. You did leave your family behind?

MAN. But I didn't forget them.

YOUNGER MAN. You didn't come back here to help strangers.

I don't think so.

We can make a lot of money brother.

I think you have more than you say. Of course you want to keep some for yourself. You are not an idiot. But if we work together, you can get even more than you imagined.

You like imagining.

Pause.

MAN. I have half a million. That's all.

I'm not trying to keep any for myself.

Perhaps I am an idiot.

But five hundred thousand pounds is everything.

Pause.

YOUNGER MAN. I don't believe you.

MAN. That's a shame.

YOUNGER MAN. What do you say brother?

An Intervention

Mike Bartlett

☞ **WHO** A and B. Their ages and genders are unspecified. (In the original production, however, A was played by a woman and B a man.)

☞ **WHERE** In front of theatre curtains like a comedy double act, though, in fact, in A's home.

☞ **WHEN** Present day.

☞ **WHAT HAS JUST HAPPENED** This duologue comes close to the start of a full-length play in which best friends A and B discuss life, love and a conflict in the Middle East. A has been on an anti-war march to protest against Britain's proposed armed intervention. B, meanwhile, supports the intervention. A is outraged at B's political stance and refusal to join the march, as a result of which the two have fallen out.

☞ **WHAT TO CONSIDER**

- We are reminded from the stage direction '*in front of theatre curtains*' of comedy double act Morecambe and Wise.

- A and B have known each other for three years.

- A is a teacher and B is a lecturer.

- Theirs is a love-hate relationship. They stimulate each other intellectually, but then they also wind each other up.

- Of their first meeting, in which they had an argument about the colour blue, A says: 'We had a great time. And realised that in the arguing we were actually quite similar. We've argued ever since. And loved it.' And B reflects: 'And from the moment we met I think we realised we did things for each other; he energised me and fired me up, and I soothed him steadied him I think and gave him perspective.' Their fall-out over Britain's decision to intervene in the Middle East, however, has changed all that.

- The exact country is not specified, though we are reminded of the civil war in Syria. Take time to research the recent crisis in the region.

- B has a girlfriend called Hannah. A hates Hannah and Hannah refuses to see A because of A's drink problem. Hannah is everything that A is not, and for a while B finds Hannah's company much more peaceful.

- The personal and the political. What happens when these clash? Decide to what extent A cannot handle loving someone whose political beliefs are so at odds with A's own. For A, B's viewpoint sheds doubt on the validity of their friendship.

- A's depression manifesting in A's drink problem. We know nothing about the root of this. Use the opportunity to create a convincing backstory for yourself.

- The exact nature of their love. How would it differ and what might it suggest if A and B were both women? Or if A was a man and B a woman, or vice versa. The play is very open to interpretation in this regard.

- Read the play to see how their relationship develops.

☞ WHAT A WANTS

- To persuade B that he is wrong.

- To make B feel his hurt and bewilderment at B's stance.

☞ WHAT B WANTS

- To defend himself.

- To get back at A for his scorn and contempt.

☞ WHAT THE SCENE IS ABOUT   Politics, conviction, disbelief, helplessness, frustration.

☞ NB   This play offers a number of other duologues from which to choose.

A *brings* B *a glass of wine.*

A   Here. An ocean of port. Now calm down.

B   Can't believe you're drinking tequila.

A   I'm not going to drink a *pint of tequila* don't be obscene. It's wine.

B   What wine?

A   Pinot. Sauvignon. Something. What are you doing?

B   You don't know which wine?

A   I'm not middle class like you.

B   I'm not expecting you to be middle class I'm expecting you to read the label.

A   Why won't you stand still?

B   Don't know what you mean.

A   Parading around.

B   Thinking.

A   Be still.

B   Is it a problem for you? If I choose to walk like this?

A   Just so long as you're relaxed.

B   All right.

       Beat.

A   Go on then.

B   *What?*

A   Relax.

B   I am.

A   doing that thing with your hand.

B   What thing?

A   Your shoulders are all

B   Well they are *now* of course they are *now* get off me! Leave me alone and I'll… *Leavemealone!*

       Beat.

A	Alright.
	Now.
	Tell me exactly why you want to invade this country and kill everyone?
B	Not me.
A	No?
B	No, *I'm* not killing anyone, if you *listened*, I'm saying I *support* –
A	Yeah but you don't have to march in there with a semi-automatic and kill the kids yourself –
B	Are you okay?
A	Yes I'm fine – you don't have to lay the illegal cluster mines with your own hands, if you're giving them support then –
B	You look a bit sad
A	Well I'm *passionate* –
B	Are those tears?
A	*This matters.*
B	No, we've talked about controversial things before, and you've never – I mean you're quite *contained* normally.
A	*Contained?* No. Contained is like the opposite of me. I don't know what you mean. Contained. Ridiculous.
B	I mean you generally don't give away how you're feeling.
A	What? I give *everything* away.
B	Well
A	I'm *Mediterranean*!
B	You – Are you?
A	Originally. You really think I'm not passionate?
B	No I didn't say not passionate
A	It's one of my *main things*.

B Yes of course, your hands waving, when you get worked up, the funny facial expressions

A Right. Exactly. Wait. Facial expressions? What facial expressions?

B Right – like that – I mean I'd assumed that it's a performance, the rolling eyes, the cheeks, because it's what you do with abstract ideas. Opinions. The tears on the other hand, like those we saw just now, only happen when it's closer to home – When it's family. Friends.

A You're saying I'm selfish now? Things only matter to me if I'm personally involved

B That's normal. If I was in a car crash you'd feel it more keenly than if it was someone else in a car crash who you never heard of.

A Hmmm I don't know, I think I'd feel a lot more sorrow for a perfectly decent stranger I hadn't previously met than the good friend, if not best friend, I unfortunately *have previously met*, who's standing in front of me calling me an alcoholic and advocating a *big war*.

B The moment you found out your mother had died, when your sister had the miscarriage

A Why are you bringing that up?

B Those are the only two moments I've seen you cry like this.

A I'm not crying.

B Despite what you think, I do know you.

A Clearly not.

B You want a hug.

A Stay away from me. Get off.

B Come on. Now you're sulking, that's the next stage.

A I'm *not* don't treat me like a child you're just trying to *distract* me from the fact you've become Hitler.

B   Okay.

A   Pol fucking *Pot*.

B   Okay.

A   Is this an experiment?

B   Hmm?

A   A kind of devil's-advocate thing like you do with your students – trying to bring out the argument in me by taking a completely *ludicrous* right-wing position?

B   Don't need to bring the argument out in you, look at you go, must be because you're *Mediterranean*

A   You really mean this neo-con shit?

B   no not neo-con but yes I do believe we have a moral obligation to go in and stop the killing yes, whatever the colour of their skin.

A   With guns.

B   If it's the only way, which I think this time, it is then yes.

        Beat.

A   Is that a moustache?

B   What?

A   Just… a trace of hair just…

B   I haven't got a clue what you're talking about.

A   (*to the audience*)

        We were meeting in Leicester Square so we could all walk down together – and it was a stupid place to meet as I'm saying it I know that we should have chosen somewhere much less crowded, but anyway eventually we got it together and the five of us were there, and I was like where is he? And they said, he never got back to us, and I was like, no no, if anyone is coming, if I would put money on *anyone* coming to attend a march against something like this, it would

be him, because, I said, he gets it, he's truly
compassionate, and you know what? I got them to
wait – I was so sure he would turn up, I got them all
to stand there for twenty minutes until they
eventually they were like 'he's really not coming' and
I looked like a prick.

B   What do you mean?

A   I mean when I was standing there waiting for you –

B   What do you mean a *moustache*?

A   I mean there's a moustache under your nose, a little
pencil-thin dictator-like, warmongering –

B   Oh okay, I get it.

    Beat.

    I didn't say I was coming. Never said that.

A   I thought I knew you well enough to assume –

B   If you'd bothered to ask –

A   Facebook?

B   If you'd actually bothered to call.

A   You should have seen it today.

B   I saw it on TV

A   You should have *been there.*

B   With the Marxists and the anti–Semites and the
islamo-fascists, and the dictator apologists, no thanks,
fine as I am.

A   Sat there on your couch

B   I wasn't *sat there* –

A   You mean you watched it *standing up*? Weird.

    I'll bet you didn't even manage that. Got bored,
    thought no one'll know, flipped it over, on with the
    porn –

B   It's me.

A   What?

B   I'm *me* here, the me you know the same me. There's things we've not agreed on before.

A   Yeah but this is different.

B *looks closely at* A.

B   I don't think it's just this that's the problem.

A   What, it's not enough? Our country goes to war because you can't be bothered to get up off your apathetic arsehole and stop it, because you'd rather sit there and crank one out

B   I wasn't 'cranking / one out'

A   rather do *whatever* you were doing than lift a finger to make a difference and you're saying that that's not enough to justify my irritation?

B   No your bottom lip tells me that the problem is much closer to home than the Middle East.

A   My bottom lip *is* the Middle East.

B   Okay – *what*?

A   That's what all of this, my face, how I'm feeling, the Middle East is entirely what it's about, nothing else.

B   I don't think that's true.

A   …

B

A   I brought the harmonica to play.

      I thought since it was a protest it might be appropriate that in some way it could maybe add to proceedings but before you ask no there was never a moment, it turned out it wasn't really that kind of thing.

B

A   What?

B   How drunk are you?

A   How does that matter?

B	I'm trying to gauge whether to bring something up or whether to leave it till the morning.
A	Four.
B	Four?
A	Yeah.
B	You seem a bit further down the…
A	Down the?
B	I mean up, up the scale, higher than four is what I'm –
A	I had one earlier and this, I've eaten dinner, I've been out all day, I've been on adrenalin not booze I'm a four. Four. Four.
B	Okay, if that's really what you think you are then –
A	Test me. Give me a word. If you don't believe me. Give me a really difficult word to say.
B	No we don't have to do that.
A	Come on, it'll be good.
B	Honorificabilitudinitatibus

Beat.

A	Is that Latin?
B	Shakespeare. Honorificabilitudinitatibus. It means –
A	Doesn't matter what it means.

A *thinks.*

Say it again.

B	Honorificabilitudinitatibus
A	Honorifica – bilitudini – bus.
B	That's actually
A	Right. Not bad. So. Four. *Four.* Means you can tell me.
B	Is it Hannah?
A	I – What?

B	Why you're crying.
A	*Hannah?*
B	Yeah. What you're really talking about tonight. Why you're – like that.

Beat.

A	*Hannah?*
B	Okay so maybe it's not.
A	*Hannah?*
B	Forget it.
A	I've been out *all day*
B	not all day
A	because I *care* because this *matters to me*, that we are about to commit to sending our troops into harm's way, *again*, and not just that, but use our bullets and bombs that *we paid for*, to kill men and woman and children in another country who have not attacked us, and I'm out there out there *all day* fighting this –
B	Not all day –
A	All *afternoon* fighting this, and I magnanimously then invite you over to my house to my flat, to defend your absence, at which point you have the gall, the huge shiny testicular *balls*, to state that all that I'm feeling, it's not to do with military intervention really. No. It's about *Hannah*.
B	It's just you don't like her very much.
A	I don't… care about her right now.
B	You've seemed a bit jealous recently.
A	I'm not getting into this. *Jealous?* Of what? No.
B	Alright maybe not jealous but you've
A	What are you talking about?
B	Since her and I have got a bit closer I think things have got more difficult between the two of us.

A   THEY HAVE NOW! This was nothing to do with that. You can do what you like. *Hannah?* You would never even ask me anything like that before today, you know I'd never stop you doing anything, I'd never tell you who to be with – you're trying to deflect away from the issue – *Hannah* isn't important, you said it probably won't last.

B   Are you sure?

A   *Yes.* What? Am I sure what?

B   That you're a four, because it was exactly this reaction that I was hoping to avoid –

A   Oh no *I'm not a four*, I *lied.* Do I *look* like a four? I can barely *stand.* I'm an *eight* at least. After the march we went to a bar and I drank a lot, but you wouldn't know that because you *weren't there* but yes I am smashed, off my trolley, off my face, I am leathered, tight, hammered and sunk. I'm a LUSH, I'm probably a nine more than an eight but if you were the person I thought you were you would know that because you would have been there today, and even if you weren't there today you'd see it in me tonight, and even if you didn't see it in me tonight, that I'm this drunk because I *care*, then we should have been able to *talk* about it, but instead you think that all this is going on because for *some reason* you've recently decided to start sleeping with and touching and generally hanging around with *Hannah* who, by the way, makes no attempt to hide her contempt for your friends, who *flirts with your mother*, and who looks like an *ant*.

B   An ant?

A   An ant yes, and yes I was a bit surprised when you two were doing things, but not nearly as surprised as today when you didn't turn up to protest with me. *This* is the problem, *what you think about this government-sanctioned act of colonial fucking terror* –

A suddenly moves and pushes B *away. It's sudden and shocks them both.*

B   Hey!

A   Sorry.

B   You… hit me –

A   I… pushed, you I know I –

B   you *hit* me.

A   Pushed. It was a push. It was like –

B   GET OFF

A   I'm *demonstrating* – Okay I'll mime it. A push is like…

    A pushes in mid-air –

    That's a push, and a hit is like –

B   What are you doing?

A   Trying to show you the difference.

B   Are you going to say sorry?

A   I… I think I already did.

    Okay.

    'Sorry.'

    Okay?

    Beat. They look at each other.

    Maybe you should go

    Before this gets any more horrorificabilitudin –

    – bus.

B   Yeah.

A   …

B   Yeah.

    Okay.

    I mean. It's late, so –

A   Just past nine not really.

B

A Sorry.

B See you then.

A Yeah.

B …

   He goes.

A Shit.

   A *sips the port.*

   Shit.

   A *looks at the harmonica.*

   Feels a bit stupid.

James II: Day of the Innocents*

Rona Munro

☞ **WHO**　William, Eighth Earl of Douglas, twenty-two years old, and James II, King of Scots, eighteen years old.

☞ **WHERE**　The Great Hall, Stirling Castle, Scotland.

☞ **WHEN**　1452.

☞ **WHAT HAS JUST HAPPENED**　William and James have been friends since boyhood. Despite the quarreling of powerful and rival factions in Scotland (and William's own father's ambition for the crown), William has remained loyal to James and has had no other desire than to be his right-hand man. However, James is troubled by William's increasingly erratic behaviour, his drunkenness and his volatility. When William's father dies, William becomes Eighth Earl of Douglas and inherits strategically important lands. His unpredictability makes the warring factions nervous. That such a potentially powerful man is so close to the King is of great concern. In order to create some stability, James appoints William his papal envoy, so sending him abroad and out of immediate reach or harm. William is furious and takes the appointment as a kind of rejection from the King. In the duologue that follows, it is six months later and William has returned to Scotland.

☞ **WHAT TO CONSIDER**

- The historical context. Take time to research this period in Scottish history.

- *James II* is the second part of a trilogy that tells the story of James the First, Second and Third of Scotland. Read all three to get a sense of the brutality inherent in this scene.

- Although events take place in the fifteenth century, the language of the play is contemporary Scots. This makes the 'story' immediate and allows us an extraordinary in to the characters' psychology and the very personal reasons for their historical actions.

* Published in the volume *The James Plays*

- Both James and William have grown up in an atmosphere of suspicion, treachery and savage violence.

- James came to the throne at six years old following the ruthless murder of his father.

- In a previous scene, William is badly beaten by his father who shows no sign of affection for his son.

- James has a large birthmark on one side of his face and was known in history as the 'fiery king'.

- Throughout the play James suffers from nightmares. He is tormented by events from the past. The killing of his father and the murder of his two friends the sixth Earl of Douglas, and his younger brother David, feature heavily in his dreams.

- The two Douglas brothers were barbarically murdered in full view of the young King when they attended a banquet where a man wearing a bull's head erupted through the table with an axe.

- After the murders James hid in a box. At the time, William was there to comfort him. Now he uses this fact to torment the King by questioning his courage.

- James and William's original closeness. The success of the scene relies heavily on the fact that these young men have had a kind of love for one another.

- James has described William as 'the dearest friend I have'.

- The play subtly suggests that William's feelings have been even more intense for James. Up until his 'banishment' he is staunchly faithful to James and is jealous when James marries and becomes a father.

- The duologue has many twists and turns. It is important that you do not pre-empt the outcome. Stay in the moment so that your audience are genuinely surprised and shocked at the ending.

- It is not until William insults James's wife and sister that James gets uncontrollably and irrevocably angrily.

☞ WHAT WILLIAM WANTS

- On the one hand, to provoke a fight, and on the other, to make his peace with James. He is conflicted.

- To punish James for having sent him away. (Decide to what extent the cruel murder of James's tax collector is part and parcel of this punishment.)

- To assert his conviction that he is the King's equal, if not his better.

- Autonomy. (Decide to what extent this is born out of his feelings of rejection by James.)

☞ WHAT JAMES WANTS

- To bring William to an understanding that he has overstepped the mark.

- To give William a chance to explain and to exonerate himself.

- To make up with William.

- To assert his manhood and his power as King.

- To protect his family.

- To avoid the kind of death of his father, who was killed in his nightshirt and unprotected.

- To rid himself of William, who by the end of the scene has become a thorn in his side.

☞ **WHAT THE SCENE IS ABOUT**   The loss of innocence (as the title suggests), a childhood friendship soured, an attempt to rekindle friendship, the will to power and the corrupting nature of power, violence that breeds violence, history repeating itself.

WILLIAM *and* JAMES *are sitting close together. They've eaten, now they're just drinking.*

WILLIAM. Everyone loves you, don't they?

JAMES. Oh, you don't?

WILLIAM. I don't mind you. I'll take a drink with you.

JAMES. Thanks. You want some more of *my* wine?

WILLIAM. In a minute.

You're popular, that's what I'm saying. You make folk smile. They think you're a good man.

JAMES. I try to be a good man.

WILLIAM. And they believe that's what you are.

It can't just be the smile, though you've got a great smile...

JAMES. I do?

WILLIAM. A boy's smile.

JAMES. A *boy's* smile?

WILLIAM. Aye. Friendly... but cheeky... a great wee boy, grinning at us all.

JAMES. Aye, well, I'm full grown, William.

WILLIAM. No, no... I'm just saying... You'll have that smile when you're sixty, man... I'm not getting at you... I'm just saying it helps folk like you.

See, I'm actually better looking than you.

JAMES. Is that right?

WILLIAM. Aye, well, you've got the... the thing there, haven't you...?

(*Indicating birthmark.*) Proof that your mother got you in a raspberry bush.

JAMES (*sarcastic*). No, the angels slapped me for leaving heaven.

WILLIAM. Ha!

Well, scrub that stain off you and you're still not a looker next to me but it does me no good. It makes folk hate me.

JAMES. Oh, is that what does it?

WILLIAM. Aye, the women hate me because they don't want to love me but they can't help themselves. The men hate me because once they've seen me their women never get wet again unless they're whispering my name. Everyone hates me.

JAMES. Because you're so good looking?

WILLIAM. It's the main reason, I'm sure of it.

See, what I'm saying is, half the badness that's said about me, half the wickedness I'm supposed to have done is no wickedness at all. It's just folk saying 'Look at that William Douglas, I hate him, he's so good looking.'

(*Starts to laugh.*) I'm joking, man, can't you tell?

This wine is shite. Why are you insulting me with the shite wine?

JAMES. That's the best we've got.

WILLIAM. It's shite. You're trying to poison me.

JAMES. I'm drinking it.

WILLIAM. Because you don't know it's shite.

JAMES. I like it.

WILLIAM. Because you're too stupid to know it's shite.

JAMES. Everyone else likes it.

WILLIAM. Because they're all feart to tell you your wine's shite. Well, I'm no feart.

JAMES. Clearly.

WILLIAM. Christ Almighty, what does it take to make you lose your temper, Jamie?

You used to have a great temper.

Used to be all you had to do was hold something up where you couldn't reach it.

Holds up food above JAMES*'s head.*

Come on, Jamie, come on, little Jamie…

JAMES. I grew up, William.

WILLIAM. You're no fun any more.

JAMES. And you're an arse.

WILLIAM. You used to like me though.

JAMES. I did. I thought you were great.

So what badness do you think folk are saying about you?

WILLIAM. I don't know.

The usual.

JAMES. What might they be saying?

WILLIAM. I don't know! You tell me!

That I'm not doing what our lovely wee King wants me to do.

JAMES. You're not sending me your taxes.

WILLIAM. Oh, listen to you. All grown up and counting money.

What do you care. You've got enough, haven't you? Maybe I just can't be bothered to gather your money in for you. Maybe I've got better things to do.

JAMES. Like killing the men I send to ask after my taxes.

WILLIAM. Oh, I only killed one of them!

Like you've never murdered a tax collector!?

JAMES. No.

WILLIAM. No, because they're your tax collectors, but take it from me, Jamie, everyone *wants* to murder a tax collector.

WILLIAM *helps himself to wine.*

I'm sorry, Jamie. I'm sorry. I never meant to fall out with you.

JAMES. Then don't. Let's fix this. Come on.

A beat.

WILLIAM. You've done as bad as me and no one hates you for it.

JAMES. How are you working that out?

WILLIAM. No, look, I'm here to apologise, alright? It's understood. It's the right thing to do, you'll hammer even more of my money off me if I don't… greedy wee shite that you are… No, but… fair enough… that aside… it's the right thing to do, plus we were always friends, we were *good* friends… I love the ghost of that wee boy grinning at me from your face there… so I do, sincerely… apologise for the wrong I've done you. Alright?

JAMES. Yes.

WILLIAM. All I'm saying is that it's not so much wrong. You've done worse. You've just got the face to get away with it.

JAMES. Well… thanks for the apology, William.

WILLIAM. I don't mean a word of it. I'm as good as you. Any day.

Can we stop this and go and get a better drink or something?

JAMES. Stop what?

WILLIAM. We're done here, aren't we? Apology on the table, you've picked it up…

I'm not going to *kneel* to you, man, so don't hold your breath waiting on that.

JAMES. What were you apologising for?

WILLIAM. Sorry?

JAMES. What were you apologising for?

WILLIAM. You don't *know*?

JAMES. I'd just be interested to know what you think you're apologising for?

WILLIAM *stares at him for a moment.*

WILLIAM. Killing your tax collector.

JAMES. You are such a piece of dog filth, man.

No, you are.

You've turned nasty. It's not funny.

WILLIAM. You heard the story, then?

JAMES. Yes.

WILLIAM. Oh, man, it was brilliant. See, I'd only *locked up* the first tax collector you sent but when Lord What's-his-face, tax collector number two, turns up, I was annoyed for a *wee* minute, can't deny it – but I made as nice as anything.

'Of course, so sorry for the wait, will you take some dinner while I fetch the money and the first tax collector you're missing?'

He's sitting waiting on his dinner. We bring it in under a cover.

(*Mimes lifting a cover.*) There's his pal's head!

WILLIAM *falls about.*

JAMES. How is that funny?

WILLIAM. It's a bit funny, though, eh?

JAMES. No.

WILLIAM. Come on, it was a bit funny. The man's face...

JAMES. No. That's not a joke.

WILLIAM. Aw, man, if you'd been there you'd've laughed, on Christ's blood I *swear* you'd have laughed...

JAMES. No.

WILLIAM (*imitates lord*). 'So where's my tax collector pal Lord What's-his-doodle?'

(*Imitates servant.*) 'Oh, he'll be here directly, sir.'

(*Uncovers a dish of food.*) Here he is!

WILLIAM *falls about.* JAMES *is just staring at him.*

Aw, come *on*, Jamie!

Alright, alright... I'm sorry. I won't kill any tax collectors ever again.

Where's the wine?

You shouldn't have sent two of them. That was just aggravation. Asking for it. You had your answer when the first boy never came home.

He's grabbed the wine and poured it.

Are you not drinking?

JAMES *says nothing, just studying him.*

Fuck that, if you're not drinking, I'm off home, either you've poisoned the stuff or you're planning on staying sober enough to stab me. Safe conduct my arse, I'm not safe unless you're as pissed as I am, *drink* will you!

JAMES *lets him fill his glass.*

And why are you looking at me like that?

He pushes away from the table.

Come on then. Come on.

JAMES. Will, what are you doing?

WILLIAM. You're after a fight. Come on then.

JAMES. Do I look like I'm after a fight?

WILLIAM. Course you're after a fight, what's wrong with you?

JAMES. Man, you came in here under safe conduct! What do you th…

WILLIAM (*cuts him off*). Aye, so did my wee cousins. Remember?

The nightmare is just coming back at the edge of JAMES's *vision. It is only there for him.*

JAMES. You're my friend. You were a friend to me that night, William, I'll never forget that.

WILLIAM. Oh, I think you will. I think you did, Jamie. You forgot all about it. Didn't you? […]

You ready to fight?

JAMES. No, I'm not ready to fight! What's wrong with you? Just shut up. Keep your nasty mouth shut.

WILLIAM. Looks to me like you might be thinking of starting that fight.

JAMES. What's wrong with you!? What's *wrong* with you?! Suppose we did fight, you're in my castle, my men, my family all round me... how do you think that would end?

WILLIAM. You threatening me, Jamie?

JAMES. I'm *not* threatening you! That's the bloody point.

I'm making up with you! Trying to. Have you noticed that yet!?

WILLIAM. You think I'm frightened of falling out with you? You think I care about that?

JAMES. No! You don't! It's fucking obvious. Hurrah for you, you're a defiant fucking hero or whatever you think you are. Why are you here, Will?

WILLIAM. You asked me here.

JAMES. And why did you come?

A beat.

WILLIAM. To let you know.

JAMES. Let me know what?

WILLIAM. That you're no better than me. And I won't be doing anything on your say-so any time soon. I just wanted to look you in the eye and say that. I think we both need to be clear about that.

JAMES. Aw, man.

Aw, man, you're a nightmare, you're a dark and stormy nightmare. What am I supposed to do with that?

WILLIAM. I don't care what you do, little Jamie.

I'm just telling you how it is.

JAMES. You've got to know I'm likely to have to kill you for saying things like that!

WILLIAM. So why am I not dead?

JAMES. I don't want to kill you, Will.

WILLIAM. Well… I got to see what dying in bed looked like, Jamie, and I'm no going like that.

No, I am not.

He gets another drink.

My dad took me round all our land a few years back. He'd got it all, all the Douglas land and more, damp patch by damp patch. Banff, Avoch, Aberdour, Moray, Strathaven, Stonehouse… Jesus… He took me over every wet, thistle-sprouting, rocky inch of it. He poked sheep and cattle he'd inherited from all my dead cousins and uncles and he laughed like a crow eating eyeballs at the fat arses on those beasts. This was him showing me how to be a rich man. Proving to me that we were rich men.

And you know what gets me?

He'd *been* to Rome. Have you been to Rome, Jamie?

JAMES. No.

WILLIAM. No.

Neither had I till you sent me. I suppose you thought you were doing me a favour?

There's a house, not a rich man's house, a wine merchant's house, an ordinary shop man's house you ride past on your way into town.

It has paintings of angels on its walls that look like a window into the next world.

It has *peacocks* in its yard. I'm not joking. The *wine merchant's* kids are kicking peacocks' eggs around his garden in Rome.

With angels watching them.

And I come home and I'm supposed to feel like a rich man because I've got another hundred wet sheep?

What's the point? Tell me? What's the point of that?

Seems to me that round here there's no point in any of it if you've got to do what another man tells you to do. Is there?

You can take my land, take all my money, have my property, go on... I'm a rich man, apparently, take the lot. Take the head off my shoulders, Jamie.

But you're never going to tell me what to do. Alright?

That's what it means to be a rich man in this country.

JAMES. So you'd like to be King.

WILLIAM. I don't want to be fucking King.

JAMES. You're a great-great-great-grandson of the Bruce. Like me. You could be King. Or would your friends not like that?

WILLIAM. What friends?

JAMES. Crawford, up Aberdeen way, remember him? MacDonald, Lord of the Isles.

I heard you were quite friendly.

WILLIAM. I don't even like them. I'm not even *talking* about that... [...]

JAMES. Well, that's funny because I heard you were dancing to Tiger Crawford's tune these days, or maybe John MacDonald's.

WILLIAM. That's still preying on your mind, is it, wee Jamie? That's got you all of a quiver, has it?

JAMES. I heard you'd made a deal with them.

WILLIAM. A deal?

JAMES. A pact then. Do you want to call it a pact? Fine, we'll call it a pact.

WILLIAM. To do what?

JAMES. Kill me. First chance you get.

A beat.

WILLIAM. You think I'd murder you?

JAMES. Oh, aye, right, push me off the throne, then. And I suppose then you'll just let me run around Stirling playing football and singing songs. That's likely, eh?

A beat.

WILLIAM. I never talked about murder. To anyone.

JAMES. Christ, man! Stop *lying* to me!

WILLIAM. I'm not lying to you.

JAMES. See, I thought that was maybe what you came to apologise about. Your little deal with Crawford and MacDonald.

Crawford to the north-east, MacDonald to the north-west, fearless wee Douglas with his radiant good looks blazing his way up from the borders… I'm a sad little hazelnut in your jaws, amn't I?

You thought I didn't know?

WILLIAM. I didn't know you listened to what they're blethering about in the kitchen, Jamie…

JAMES. So it's not true?

WILLIAM. I don't know what's in another man's head. Crawford and MacDonald can think what they like. Doesn't mean I'll dance to their tune any more than yours. And I never talked about murder. All the rest… you brought on yourself when you decided to show the world you were master of me, Jamie. You're not. You never will be.

JAMES. So it's true.

What's in it for you, Will, a *thousand* more wet sheep? I thought you were above all that grubbing about for land and money. Isn't that what you were just telling me? So why do you want my crown, Will?

WILLIAM. I don't. I've my own power, wee King. Better than yours. All you need to know is that you don't tell Douglas what to do. Ever.

JAMES. You've made a deal with my enemies. You've killed my servants. You're plotting to kill me.

WILLIAM. Are you asking me now or telling me?

JAMES. *Why?*

A beat.

WILLIAM. Fight me.

JAMES. What?

WILLIAM. Just… Come on… *fuck* you, James… come on
then! If that's what you think… Come on! We'll fix this
then. Fight me!

Look, I'll make it easy for you, no blades, eh?

WILLIAM *slams his knife into the table.*

Just have a go at beating my brains out. We'll do it that
way.

Come on!! You and me! You and me!

JAMES. *There's no you and me, Will!* You killed it!
Understand?!

That's gone now.

Done.

A stand-off for a moment.

WILLIAM. Aw Jesus…

*The bull-headed man moves through the shadows in the room,
streaked with blood. James can see him, no one else can.*

Well, you better have me executed then, James, eh? Since
I'm that fucking dangerous, since I'm in here, a king killer,
in here, with his King. Better call for some help, James, eh?
Because if that's who I am there's no hope, is there? No
hope for any of us.

If I'd wanted to murder you I could've strangled you in
your sleep, Jamie, couldn't I? You always slept deep when I
was keeping watch over you after all. Keeping the
nightmares away from you.

JAMES. You murdered my men! You're planning war against
me!

WILLIAM. Aye, right enough, right enough, what was I
thinking? I don't even know why I came to talk to you.

You're right. We're done now.

You still have nightmares, James?

I think you still have nightmares.

You're right. I'm your nightmare.

How are you going to send me away? Eh? How are you going to do that, wee Jamie?

WILLIAM *goes to get himself another drink.*

JAMES. You said you were my friend.

WILLIAM. Oh, the *bairn.* Listen to him!

I am your friend. It's good we're having this talk. You need to know what you're up against. I won't be ruled. Everyone needs to know. Douglas has made his mind up. He's made his mind up to do whatever Douglas pleases till he dies.

Aye. If you try and tell me what to do I will bring you war, Jamie.

If *anyone* tries to tell me what to do I'll bring war, Jamie. I can raise an army any time I want.

But maybe I won't. I like you. Live quiet and I'll maybe leave you alone, little red face.

(*Moving closer to him.*) As long as we *both* know that any time I liked… *any* time I liked I could just walk in here, stamp on your bairn's head, slice your wife's throat and fuck your sister on the floor in front of you and you couldn't raise a finger to stop me. As long as we both know that.

Actually, that sounds like a plan. Shall I do that? Or maybe I'll slice your bairn, stamp on your sister's head and fuck your wife? She looks like a better shag to me. Is she?

(*Laughs.*) Oh, don't look at me like that! I'm only messing with you. I won't hurt you, wee boy. Tell you what, seeing as you're so scared shall we get you a wee box to hide in? Would that help?

(*Points.*) Shall we use that one? Aye, why don't we do that? You get in the box and put your fingers in your ears and I'll shag your pretty wee wife. Is that a plan? Just get in the box, Jamie, you like that, don't you? You feel safe in your wee box, eh? Get in the box.

He's moving his face closer and closer to JAMES.

Get in the box.

Get in the box!

Get in…

Before he can finish the sentence JAMES *has knocked him down. He grabs the knife and stabs* WILLIAM *twice.*

WILLIAM *screams.*

JAMES *steps back.*

WILLIAM *is struggling on the floor, shocked and bleeding. He's not quite dead. It's all been horribly quick.*

WILLIAM *makes a horrible blood-choked noise and struggles to get up.* JAMES *instantly rushes at him again kicking, punching, stabbing him to death.*

Jumpers for Goalposts

Tom Wells

☞ **WHO**   Danny, twenty-two, and Luke, nineteen.

☞ **WHERE**   A football changing room in Hull. (If you are not from Hull, you may like to play the scene in your own accents.)

☞ **WHEN**   Present day.

☞ **WHAT HAS JUST HAPPENED**   Danny and Luke play for an amateur five-a-side football team. Danny is on a sports training placement, Luke is a librarian. Both men are gay and fancy each other, but neither until now has been brave enough to make the first move. In the duologue that follows, they have been celebrating the birthday of one of their team members. They are now on their own, and Luke is finishing a can of Guinness.

☞ **WHAT TO CONSIDER**

- Danny first met Luke in the library where he convinced him to come and play football. However, the team they play for, 'Barely Athletic', are, as their name suggests, pretty hopeless.

- Luke is scared, and, as we will later discover, Danny is HIV positive. It is little wonder they are so awkward with one another.

- The play is a comedy but also deeply affecting. It is important that you do not play the scene just for laughs or send it up in any way.

☞ **WHAT DANNY WANTS**

- To kiss Luke.
- To reassure Luke.
- To be with Luke.

☞ **WHAT LUKE WANTS**

- For Danny to kiss him.
- To take things slowly.
- To feel comfortable with his own sexuality.

☞ **WHAT THE SCENE IS ABOUT**   Coming of age, overcoming fears, the need for intimacy, relief at discovering you are not alone.

☞ **NB**   This play offers a number of other duologues from which to choose.

DANNY. Come to the pub one night. [...]

LUKE. Maybe. I dunno actually, I don't really. I'm not very pubby to be honest. I'm more sort of, stay-in-on-my-own-y. With a book or. Don't even drink that much normally. I mean not that, this is, yeah –

DANNY. Don't have to drink it if you don't want.

LUKE. I didn't want to waste it.

DANNY. I'll finish it.

LUKE. What about driving?

DANNY. Only half a can isn't it? Be fine.

LUKE wipes the top of the can with his sleeve.

What you doing?

LUKE. Just wiping the spit off.

He gives the can to DANNY. DANNY is smiling.

What?

DANNY. Nothing. Cheers.

LUKE. Why you smiling?

DANNY. Dunno, you're funny.

LUKE sighs.

What's up?

LUKE. Nothing. Just feel like I keep making a massive tit of myself, it's a bit…

DANNY. Not massive.

LUKE nods, smiles, a bit sad.

LUKE. We should, um.

DANNY. What?

LUKE. Um. Sweep?

DANNY. Oh, yeah.

LUKE. D'you want to do it yourself? The sweeping? Don't want to get it wrong.

DANNY. You won't get it wrong.

LUKE. I probably will.

DANNY. Luke.

LUKE. Honestly, I can get anything wrong. It's like a superpower.

> DANNY *touches* LUKE *on the shoulder.* LUKE *looks up.*

DANNY. Um.

LUKE. What's…?

DANNY. Nothing just. Just wondered if. I just.

LUKE. What?

DANNY. Um. I'd really like to kiss you, Luke. If that's…

LUKE. Are you sure?

> DANNY *laughs. Nods.*
>
> *They kiss. It's a gentle one.*
>
> *A moment.* LUKE *laughs.*

DANNY. What?

LUKE. Taste of, thingy.

> DANNY *laughs.*

DANNY. Soz.

LUKE. No it's, nice.

DANNY. Oh now it's nice.

> *A moment.*
>
> You alright?

LUKE. Yeah I'm fine. Think I'm just a bit.

> LUKE *breathes out.*

You know.

DANNY. Sure?

LUKE. We should get off. Home. We should be getting off home.

DANNY. It's alright.

LUKE. Your assignment though.

DANNY. It's fine. Are you worried?

LUKE. No just –

DANNY. Yorkshire puddings.

LUKE. No. Well, yeah but.

DANNY. We can still make it back before –

LUKE. Don't even like them to be honest. My dad's anyway. They're shit. It's cos: my mum's favourite, Yorkshire puddings. But then she cooks everything all week so my dad just sort of decided he'd do Sunday dinner but, as a gesture but, thing is, he's so shit, my mum ends up doing it all anyway. He just does the Yorkshire puddings. Badly. But then he is weirdly precious about it.

Deep breath.

Sorry this has thrown me a bit. I mean I was already, got my top and I was like: oh my God I'm actually on a team. With a nickname. That's like, appropriate. Cos it's. Not really had one before, normally just, people in the past just went for sort of, Bender, whatever. But: a snog! That is, even better. Honestly. And it's, yeah. First one, actually. I know: pathetic, like I'm all, I'm nineteen but. I'm from Patrington, work in a library it's. Slim pickings, if I'm honest. Cos, can't snog a book, can you? My mum said that. Well, she said you can but, they don't snog back. Which is actually just, you know. The truth.

DANNY. Just a little kiss, Luke.

LUKE. I know.

DANNY. You can have another.

126

LUKE. I'd love that.

DANNY *laughs.*

DANNY. Come here.

He pulls LUKE *towards him, kisses him. Tender. Starts to take* LUKE*'s top off, gently.* LUKE *jumps, moves away. Quick.*

You alright?

LUKE. Yeah, yeah.

DANNY. What's up?

LUKE. Nothing. I dunno.

DANNY. You sure?

LUKE. Yeah.

A moment.

DANNY. Sorry.

LUKE. No.

DANNY. Got a bit –

LUKE. Yeah, no.

DANNY *smiles.*

DANNY. Worried I'll peep?

LUKE. Not much to look at.

DANNY. Probably would peep though. To be honest.

LUKE *wrinkles his nose.*

A moment.

Take it off?

LUKE *shakes his head.*

Only me.

LUKE. Exactly.

DANNY. Take mine off an' all.

LUKE. It's not that.

DANNY. Or, maybe, you could take mine off?

LUKE. Nah.

DANNY. Well, it's coming off.

DANNY *takes his top off. Smiles.*

There. Your go.

LUKE. I'm really not –

DANNY. Your go, Luke.

LUKE *takes his first top off.*

One down.

LUKE. Danny –

DANNY. I get it, you're shy, I know. And, like, you don't have to. If you don't want to. But I think maybe you want to.

DANNY *touches the bottom of* LUKE's *second top.* LUKE *holds it down.*

LUKE. You have to promise not to take the piss.

DANNY *(gently)*. Come on then.

DANNY *takes* LUKE's *top off.*

He's got a thermal vest on underneath. Tucked into his shorts.

Fucking hell, Luke.

LUKE. Don't.

DANNY. A vest though? A real-life thermal vest.

LUKE. Thing is: I just, I feel the cold. Get really chilly so, thought, you know. Layers.

Regretting it now.

DANNY *is smiling.*

What?

DANNY. Nothing just. Think I just fell in love. A bit.

LUKE *doesn't know what to say.*

Wondering: this week if we could. If you were free one night we could maybe sort of, do, something?

LUKE. Yeah I'm, I'm free. Every night.

LUKE *looks worried.*

DANNY. Sure you're alright?

LUKE. Thing is, I'm actually. I'm a bit of a nervous gay so.

DANNY. No?

LUKE. So if we could just sort of go, steady that'd be. Slow even, that'd be…

DANNY. Taken us three months to manage a snog, Luke, think we've set quite a good pace.

A moment.

LUKE *smiles.*

LUKE. Two snogs.

DANNY *smiles.*

DANNY. Three?

DANNY *goes in for another kiss.* LUKE *stops him.*

LUKE. Football.

That's what we can do. In the week. Help me get better at football.

DANNY. Do my best.

Kiss.

Lizzie Siddal

Jeremy Green

☞ **WHO**   Charles Howell and Dante Gabriel Rossetti.

☞ **WHERE**   Rossetti's house in Chelsea, London.

☞ **WHEN**   10th February, 1869, night-time.

☞ **WHAT HAS JUST HAPPENED**   The following duologue comes at the end of the play. It is seven years since Rossetti's wife, Lizzie Siddal, committed suicide, and Rossetti's agent thinks it is about time Rossetti retrieved the poems that he had buried with his wife's body.

☞ **WHAT TO CONSIDER**

- The play tells the real-life story of Lizzie Siddal and the Brotherhood of 'Pre-Raphaelite' artists for whom she was a model.

- She is most famously remembered for posing as 'Ophelia' in a painting by Millais. She became seriously ill after lying for hours on end in a bath of freezing cold water.

- Read the whole play and take time to do your own research into this revolutionary period in Art History.

- A year into their marriage, Lizzie gave birth to a stillborn child. She never recovered from the loss and, a year later, addicted to laudanum, she took an overdose and died. She was thirty-two.

- When she was buried, Rossetti buried his poems with her.

- It is fair to say that Lizzie was far more in love with Rossetti than he was with her. She was his muse, however, and appeared in many of his famous works. Decide to what extent his declaration of love, by burying his poems with her, was born more out of guilt than true love.

- Lizzie was an artist in her own right. Although her talent was largely dismissed by the Brotherhood, Rossetti was keen to encourage her. In a previous scene he defends Lizzie's work.

- Charles Howell, Rossetti's agent, appears only twice in the play. In the first scene, where he goes to perform the exhumation, and here in the last scene that sees him convincing Rossetti of the right to do so. Take time to research the real-life man. He was a renowned liar and swindler and yet immensely charming.

☞ WHAT HOWELL WANTS

- To gain Rossetti's approval of his plan.
- To make money.
- To feed off the talent of others in order to further his own reputation.

☞ WHAT ROSSETTI WANTS

- Praise.
- Fame.
- Glory. (Note how impressed he is by Howell's suggestion that the publication of his poems will bring him 'immortality'.)

☞ WHAT THE SCENE IS ABOUT   Art as a business, exploitation, vanity and narcissism, the emotional cost to the women who love 'great' men.

Night. A house in Chelsea. The (sound of) knocking. [...]

HOWELL (*off*). Gabriel? It's me, Charlie Howell. I'm dying out here. I'm not joking. In fact, I may already be dead. This may be my ghost talking...

ROSSETTI *enters.* [...] *He carries a candle, walks across the room, places the candle down.*

Gabriel? Can you open the door, please, it's cold, I mean, really freezing, I've just lost a testicle. It froze and dropped off. Look, there it goes now rolling down the street.

ROSSETTI *exits towards the noise.*

It's Charles Howell, Gabriel – your agent. I want to talk to you, for pity's sake.

Offstage, a door opens.

My dear chap, thank God. I can't shake hands just now, my fingers would break.

I could be the first man to die of frostbite in Chelsea.

HOWELL *walks in, followed by* ROSSETTI.

It's very dark in here. Where's your housekeeper?

ROSSETTI. I gave her the night off.

HOWELL. Where's the fire? Aren't you cold?

ROSSETTI. I am cold, yes.

HOWELL. Shall I light a fire?

ROSSETTI. No. I want to feel cold.

HOWELL. What's wrong? What? Something is. You've been shut up in here for a month. What's different? I don't smell any paint. Are you not painting?

ROSSETTI. No.

HOWELL. Why not?

ROSSETTI. It's too cold.

HOWELL.…(*the penny drops*). Oh Lord. It's the tenth. Tonight is the tenth.

ROSSETTI. Yes.

HOWELL. My dear chap.

ROSSETTI. Yes.

HOWELL. How could I not remember? Heavens, you must feel so – How can one put it in words?…

ROSSETTI.   'Then black despair,
     The shadow of a starless night, was thrown
     Over the world in which I moved alone.'

HOWELL. I say, that's terrific. Did you write that?

ROSSETTI. No. Shelley.

HOWELL. Oh, of course, Shelley – wonderful poet. You poor fellow, how long is it – six? – seven years ago tonight she passed away. You must feel such grief. Well, never you mind what I came for – I shan't even say.

ROSSETTI. Say what?

HOWELL. I shan't say, not now… Although if you really want to know. I suppose you do want to know. Well, if you must know, I came to talk poetry.

ROSSETTI. Poetry?

HOWELL. Yes.

ROSSETTI. I have no poetry.

HOWELL. No.

ROSSETTI. I buried most of my poems in her coffin.

HOWELL. You did. Yes. Your only copy, handwritten – extraordinary thing to do.

ROSSETTI. And now I can't remember them.

HOWELL. No. Might as well not have written them. Anyway, who cares about poems? You poor, poor man. What agonies you must be suffering. I won't even tell you my gossip.

ROSSETTI. Don't. I hate gossip.

HOWELL. So do I. I won't mention Coventry Patmore.

ROSSETTI. Patmore? What about him?

HOWELL. Bell have signed Patmore to bring out a new volume of verse.

ROSSETTI. Patmore?

HOWELL. Yes.

ROSSETTI. He writes twaddle.

HOWELL. Yes. Good twaddle though; sells well…

> 'And she assumed the maiden coy,
> And I adored remorseless charms,
> And then we clapp'd our hands for joy,
> And ran into each other's arms.'

ROSSETTI. For the love of Christ!

HOWELL. Sorry… Anyway, you're right – Patmore – not exactly Shelley. Now *there's* a writer – Shelley. *His* book will live for ever. And was it really seven years ago you took *your* book of poems – your only copy – and placed it in Lizzie's coffin? Some would question the sense of that.

ROSSETTI. Let them. I wanted to show her how much I loved her.

HOWELL. Yes. Although. She was already dead.

ROSSETTI. She killed herself.

HOWELL. The coroner said 'accidental death'. Unless you know something.

Pause.

Were there any love poems? In the book? The book you put in her coffin? Any love poems?

ROSSETTI. I can't remember.

HOWELL. Only, love poems are very popular just now… It is a shame to have a talent like yours write poems that will never be read. Patmore is read. Rossetti is not. It seems to me a terrible tragedy that Lizzie, who loved poetry, should be the very cause now of concealing it.

ROSSETTI. Well. That is how it is.

HOWELL. Not quite… I've made enquiries. It turns out the book could be recovered.

ROSSETTI. What?

HOWELL. People sometimes bury things, then change their minds, and want them back.

ROSSETTI. D'you mean… dig her up?

HOWELL. The word they use is 'un-coffined'. I know it sounds ghastly, but apparently it's perfectly / normal.

ROSSETTI. No!… Good God!

Pause.

HOWELL. No one would ever know.

ROSSETTI. I would know.

HOWELL. Yes. You would know and I would know, but no one else... Well, a chaplain would have to be present... And a lawyer... And the gravediggers... And the Secretary for the Home Office would need to sign the papers; though I am persuaded that's a formality for an artist of your prominence. And there's a man I know can disinfect the book. Total cost: two pounds two shillings. A small price to pay for / your poetry.

ROSSETTI. There is no question of opening her grave. No question.

HOWELL. Right... It's a 'no'. Then I shall not mention it again... Your neighbour's tree was full of icicles just now.

ROSSETTI. She loved my poetry.

HOWELL. We might all love it, Gabriel, if we could but read it.

ROSSETTI. We can't.

HOWELL. We could.

ROSSETTI. Disturb her grave?

HOWELL. We're not disturbing a person. She's dead. They're your poems.

ROSSETTI. It is unthinkable.

HOWELL. It's not.

ROSSETTI. Understand this, Charlie. To sanction such an act is not within my philosophy. You would have to find some other Rossetti. No poet, no artist, no human being, no man that I would recognise as party to myself would ever do such a thing.

HOWELL. I understand. The Romantic Soul. It does you credit. Though I do think you ought to spare a thought for Lizzie's wishes in this matter. She who loved poetry. What would *she* want? Would she wish to be the cause your poems are unread, unregarded, unremembered... underground? No. No. Could she open the grave herself, my hand would not be needed.

ROSSETTI. You truly think that?

HOWELL. I do. Your best work buried, and to what purpose?

ROSSETTI. I really think it might have been my best work.

HOWELL. So do I.

ROSSETTI. You think she'd want me to?

HOWELL. I know she would.

ROSSETTI. But what if it leaked out?

HOWELL. It won't.

ROSSETTI. But if it did? Would there not be some stain on me? Would it not be seen as vanity on my part?

HOWELL. Talent vindicates all behaviour. The work is more important than the details of a life. No one remembers the life, it's the legacy that counts. Did Shakespeare bury his book? No. Did Dante? No. Your immortality lies just beneath the turf. I can retrieve it. Just say the word... Say yes... Or nod your head... That's all it takes. A nod... Just a nod.

ROSSETTI *makes no sign. He does not nod his head.*

I saw a nod. Then. I did. You nodded. It's all right, it's done, it's over. I have the papers with me. Oh. I need one signature. Do you have a pen?

ROSSETTI. In the next room.

HOWELL. You won't regret this. I promise. Shall we?

ROSSETTI. If it ever got out.

HOWELL. It won't. It won't.

ROSSETTI *turns.*

ROSSETTI. I still turn round sometimes, expecting to see her.

HOWELL. Gabriel. Immortality. It's this way.

ROSSETTI *picks up the candle and the two of them leave.*

Mad About the Boy

Gbolahan Obisesan

☞ **WHO**   Boy, fourteen, black/mixed-race/Asian, and Man, late-twenties/early thirties, white/black/mixed-race/Asian.

☞ **WHERE**   Unspecified. We assume in a room at the boys' school.

☞ **WHEN**   Present day.

☞ **WHAT HAS JUST HAPPENED**   The Boy has been threatened with exclusion from school for having punched a supply teacher. His father is unable to control him and one option is that he should go into foster care. Meanwhile, in the hope that something can be done about his anti-social behaviour and before he is sent to a pupils' referral unit, it is agreed that he should have counselling. In the duologue that follows, the Man attempts to help the Boy.

☞ **WHAT TO CONSIDER**

- The play is a three-hander. It tells the story of an inner-city boy who has been seduced by gang culture, his father who struggles to cope, and the school counsellor who wishes to help. The three characters are known only as Boy, Dad and Man. Apart from their ages, ethnicity and key events in their lives, the writer tells us only a few facts about them. The writing, however, is so strong that we feel we know them. Use the blanks in the story to develop fully rounded characters for yourselves, creating precise and detailed back stories.

- The Man can be from an educated, working-class background. Although the play is written in the Boy's vernacular, the Man's accent and way of speaking is close to that of the Boy's.

- The Man was in foster care as a child.

- The Boy has been hit by his father as a way of disciplining him. To what extent has this use of violence influenced the Boy's behaviour and muddled the distinction between what is right and wrong?

- The death of the Boy's mother. In his mind the very fact of him killed her. To what extent does this skewed association feed into his views on women in general and to his own notion of himself as a killer?

- Arguably, the Man is not clever enough for the Boy, and in this way fails him.

☞ WHAT THE BOY WANTS

- To face up to the Man and to get in first. (Note the way he taunts the Man by pre-empting the Man's suggestion that he 'could find a better way – a better solution to the decisions you need to make', by telling him: 'You've got no ambition – you're a giver-rup-per', and again: 'Just trying to give you more options – make you ambitious.')

- Attention. (Note how he likes to shock and to cause offence. To what extent is this a front to shield him from painful and vulnerable sensations? The boy is conflicted. On the one hand, he wants to please his father and to do right by the Man, but on the other, he wants the feeling of belonging and respect he gets from being part of the gang.)

☞ WHAT THE MAN WANTS

- To educate the boy.

- To change his limiting and limited view of the world – to be his 'attitude-adjuster'.

- To help. To what extent does his own experience of hardship create a compulsion or an obligation in him to help others?

- To head off the boy before he commits a serious offence or gets himself killed.

☞ WHAT THE SCENE IS ABOUT   The failure of the school system to have any real influence on the after-school lives of boys who are in gangs, the difference between the generations (the Man, who has a certain respect for the law, and the Boy, who is seemingly fearless of authority), frustration, hopelessness, helplessness.

☞ NB   This play offers another duologue between the Boy and his dad.

BOY. What do you know about girls?

MAN. What do I know – ?

BOY. About girls.

MAN. About girls?

BOY. You're not deaf.

MAN. I know I'm not deaf.

BOY. Then why are you carrying on like Beethoven –

MAN. I don't think I should – How do you know he was deaf?

BOY. Why? – Shouldn't I know?

MAN. It's not that you shouldn't know – just wondering how you do?

BOY. I just do.

MAN. You just do –

BOY. yeah –

MAN. Fine…

BOY. He went deaf in his twenties, but carried on making music –

MAN. That's right –

BOY. He felt it –

MAN. Definitely –

BOY. I like music you can feel –

MAN. Like?

BOY. Anything as long as I feel it –

MAN. Tell the girl –

BOY. what?

MAN. Tell her –

BOY. tell her I feel music –

MAN. Yeah – why not?

BOY. I want to feel her that's why –

MAN. She might be feeling you if you tell her something
about yourself –

BOY. That's moist –

MAN. What's that?

BOY. It's weak – I ain't weak.

MAN. Stop being wet –

BOY. I'm trying to get her wet –

MAN. You got no respect –

BOY. and –

MAN. where's your respect?

BOY. What you talking about?

MAN. respect – ?

BOY. respect what?

MAN. Her, the girl –

BOY. why?

MAN. because you like her –

BOY. So?

MAN. So it's just nice –

BOY. But I'm not nice – I mean – I'm *nice* like buff, but not
nice like spice –

MAN. girls like nice –

BOY. Not all girls like nice –

MAN. No not all girls –

BOY. So I'll go for the ones that don't like that nice –

MAN. no girl's never not liked nice –

BOY. This is confusing – what are you saying?

MAN. It's complicated –

BOY. why do you have to make it complicated – ?

MAN. Girls like – Women like nice and some *like* – as you
say, prefer *nice* –

BOY. Buff nice –

MAN. Yeah, but some might not even be nice –

BOY. Ugly.

MAN. Yes – No – I mean – I meant – soft – hardened women

BOY. Hard women?

MAN. Yeah. Some hard women still like nice men

BOY. what like Peter Andre?

MAN. I don't know – maybe.

BOY. I ain't no Peter Andre though –

MAN. No?

BOY. Ain't. no. Peter. Andre. –

MAN. Okay you're not Peter Andre

BOY. As long as you know –

MAN. I know now –

BOY. You done know –

MAN. I know now you're not Peter Andre, but some women like that sort of nice and under the circumstances – this girl you like might be one of those types of women and if she's as nice as you've made her to be, she might also be a girl that's nice to other women –

BOY. lesbians –

MAN. Yes – which means they're not nice for you –

BOY. You mean I'm not nice to them –

MAN. Exactly – so they won't fancy you –

BOY. You think she's lesbian?

MAN. No I never said that –

BOY. But you're suggesting –

MAN. That not all girls are gonna like you –

BOY. Because they're lesbian –

MAN. No – probably because they don't think you're nice –

BOY. But I am nice –

MAN. Maybe not as nice to them as you might like –

BOY. Alright I hear that… but what if I find a nice girl that the lesbian thinks is nice and because the nice girl thinks I'm nice, the lesbian girl then starts to think uh actually he's quite nice and she wants me and the nice girl and her to nice up their sheets with all our wetness like one big paddling pool –

MAN. That might never happen –

BOY. Maybe not to you

MAN. You've got to be realistic.

BOY. but. what. if. it. did –

MAN. It's unlikely –

BOY. why's it unlikely?

MAN. because your nice girl might just go off with the other nice girl –

BOY. The lesbian –

MAN. the lesbian – because your nice girl thinks the other girl is nicer and no longer thinks you or guys are nice –

BOY. that's not nice though is it –

MAN. it's just the way things are sometimes –

BOY. I don't want sometime-ish – I want my bit whenever I want it –

MAN. we don't always get what we want when we want it –

BOY. You might not –

MAN. What does that mean?

BOY. Exactly what it is.

MAN. If I know I can't have it I forget about it –

BOY. That's waste –

MAN. Maybe –

BOY. You're a waste, man –

142

MAN. I don't know what you mean –

BOY. You've got no ambition – you're a giver-rup-per

MAN. I'm not –

BOY. Don't sound like it –

MAN. I understand what it sounds like, but that's not the reality –

BOY. so what's the reality?

MAN. It just. Sometimes we ain't always in control, but the bit that we are in control of we want it to run smoothly –

BOY. Do you think you're in control right now?

MAN. I'm trying to maintain control –

BOY. maintain – hold on to – you can't hold me.

MAN. You're obligated to be here –

BOY. Yeah, it's my school – why are you here?

MAN. I'm the school counsellor –

BOY. So what –

MAN. so what.

BOY. so what if you wasn't?

MAN. but I am, it's my job.

BOY. What if you wasn't – you had another job – the job you've always wanted…

MAN. another job?

BOY. You've always wanted…

MAN. …an artist –

BOY. what?

MAN. maybe an artist –

BOY. Artist?

MAN. Yes artist –

BOY. That's waste – they don't do shit –

MAN (*laughs*). You asked –

BOY. Politician!

MAN. don't make me laugh –

BOY. Just trying to give you more options – make you ambitious –

MAN. A politician?

BOY. Yeah you could be a good politician –

MAN. A good politician?

BOY. You like telling people what to do don't you –

MAN. It's not –

BOY. Look – If you want people to listen to you – you put them in their place – (*Gesturing with finger pointed downwards with attitude.*) and tell them what to do –

MAN. You like telling people what to do.

BOY. That's what I'm saying – I was born to tell people what to do –

MAN. So you could be a good politician.

BOY. Spending all that money on wars and holiday homes and shit like that – Hell yeah –

MAN. That's a bad politician –

BOY. Not if it's what I have to do –

MAN. You could find a better way – a better solution to the decisions you need to make –

BOY. What – Like – hide it from people?

MAN. That would make you a really bad politician –

BOY. But isn't that just being smart?

MAN. a smart politician would find the right way to do the job properly in the first place –

BOY. It don't matter anyway, they've let in Obama now so the door's shut for say fifty years –

MAN. President of America might not work anyway –

BOY. Why?

MAN. Cos you're not American – Prime Minister on the other hand –

BOY. That won't work either –

MAN. why not?

BOY. Do I look English?

MAN. That's not the correct attitude to have –

BOY. You're not a politician so you can't tell me what sort of attitude to have –

MAN. I've been placed here by our current best politicians to be your attitude-adjuster –

BOY. If you want me to adjust my attitude – tell me how to get the girl I like to give me head –

MAN. …If that's all you want her for, then why should she?

BOY. She should because she's a sket –

MAN. what?

BOY. a jezzie –

MAN. je– what?

BOY. Slit

MAN. Woh –

BOY. Cunt –

MAN. pardon –

BOY. Shinners –

MAN. Stop –

BOY. Knob polisher –

MAN. Can you –

BOY. Porridge pot –

MAN. Stop –

BOY. Spunk bucket –

MAN. that's enough –

BOY. waste basket –

MAN. THAT'S ENOUGH –

BOY. that's what I think –

MAN. You can't talk about –

BOY. what?

MAN. About women like that –

BOY. who says?

MAN. women – I say –

BOY. Like I care what anyone thinks –

MAN. What if someone spoke about your sister like that –

BOY. I ain't got no sister –

MAN. For the sake of argument –

BOY. I ain't arguing –

MAN. Then you've got a sister –

BOY. No I ain't –

MAN. This girl you're talking about – anyhow – she is your sister?

BOY. No she's not.

MAN. But what if she was?

BOY. But she's not –

MAN. she's not but she could be.

BOY. I don't see how she could be, because she's not

MAN. hypothetically –

BOY. Hypo– what?

MAN. Let's imagine – Let's suppose – let's imagine

BOY. Imagine what?

MAN. That this girl is you sister.

BOY. Why you saying that – why are you doing that?

MAN. If she was your sister –

BOY. she's not – stop it –

MAN. would you still like – Other boys talking –

BOY. why are you still talking?

MAN. look at her like –

BOY. Like man would fuck his own sister –

MAN. undressing her – doing – saying disrespectful –

BOY. disrespecting man's right to want woman –

MAN. misogyny – that's what it's called –

BOY. You must miss ogling –

MAN. Ogling?

BOY. I bet –

    You must like ogling –

MAN. Ogling? – I don't do ogling –

BOY. Take a mental picture do you – Hold it in for your spank bank?

MAN. what?

BOY. Tell me you don't spank – errh you spank.

MAN. I don't think that's appropriate –

BOY. I don't think what you're saying is appropriate.

MAN. what if she was your mother?

BOY. My mother's dead – I killed her.

MAN. What?

BOY. You heard –

MAN. What makes you think you killed her?

BOY. because I did –

MAN. How is that possible?

BOY. I ruptured her punani –

MAN. I don't understand?

BOY. I collapsed her pussy –

MAN. Is that a figure of speech?

BOY. That's what happened.

MAN. how could that have happened –

BOY. It just did.

MAN. To your own mother?

BOY. When she had me – she bled to death – Done.

MAN. I wish you wouldn't –

BOY. wouldn't tell the truth –

MAN. No – be so graphic

BOY. I'm a graphic maverick –

MAN. graphic maverick?

BOY. Larger-than-life rebel –

MAN. you revel in that don't you.

BOY. that's why people like me.

MAN. People don't like you – the girl doesn't like you.

BOY. chatting shit –

MAN. think about it –

BOY. why you saying that?

MAN. it's the truth.

BOY. I don't wanna hear that –

MAN. It's important –

BOY. Who's been talking foolishness?

MAN. It's not foolishness – you need to find out why they don't like you?

BOY. I need to know who they are, so I can kill them.

MAN. …Kill them?

BOY. Make their head trickle – slosh poppies –

MAN. let's not rush our thoughts – not make hasty conclusions

BOY. fuck this –

The Maths Tutor

Clare McIntyre

☞ **WHO**   Tom, fifteen, and JJ, fifteen.

☞ **WHERE**   On the street riding mountain bikes. (The duologue works equally well with the boys just walking.)

☞ **WHEN**   Present day. (The play was first performed in 2003 and I would suggest changing some of the film references in order to update it.)

☞ **WHAT HAS JUST HAPPENED**   JJ and Tom are best friends. They go to different schools but share the same after-school maths tutor. JJ's parents are divorced and JJ's mother is having an affair with a much younger man, whom JJ hates. JJ is angry about the situation and in a misplaced act of revenge he makes up a story about how Brian, the maths tutor, has sexually assaulted him. In this duologue, JJ attempts to get Tom to share in the lie.

☞ **WHAT TO CONSIDER**

- JJ's rage and depression is largely to do with the fact that his parents are not together.

- Tom's parents seem to have the perfect relationship, but as we discover in the duologue, Tom's father is gay, and we later find out that their marriage has been a sham.

- Tom's parents have no idea that Tom knows his dad is gay. They have been keeping it from him to 'protect' him, but have, in effect, been lying to him.

- JJ is spoilt. He has more money spent on him than Tom. His bike is flashier and he goes to a more expensive school. However, it is important that you do not judge him. His bad behaviour is rooted in his unhappiness, and it is important that we feel sympathy for him.

- On the surface, Tom is much nicer than JJ. He is considerate, highly intelligent and sensitive. Whatever their problems, he is adored by his parents and enjoys their company.

- The boys are best friends but are also competitive with one another. JJ often tries to put Tom down, and Tom knows how to retaliate. Note how Tom calls JJ stupid – we know from an earlier scene that this infuriates him.

- 'The big deal' is the fact that JJ's mother believes JJ's story about Brian and is giving JJ extra treats because she feels bad about what happened.

- In a previous scene, JJ was showing off and gave Tom the impression that he had slept with a girl called Monica. JJ is manipulative and he now uses this as a means of getting closer to Tom by admitting to having lied about it; something that he says he would only share with a best friend. To what extent is he trying to sweeten Tom up before eliciting his help?

- Jane is Tom's mother.

☞ WHAT TOM WANTS

- To stand up to JJ.
- To act honestly. Make a decision about whether his desire for honesty is because he has seen his dad living a lie.

☞ WHAT JJ WANTS

- Tom's help.
- Attention. He is very threatened by his mother's new relationship. Because his mother believes that he has been sexually abused, she is giving JJ much more of her time.

☞ WHAT THE SCENE IS ABOUT   Power struggle within friendship, manipulation, resistance, the power children can have over adults in a paranoid world.

☞ NB   This play offers a number of other duologues from which to choose.

TOM *and* JJ *are on mountain bikes.* JJ*'s is flashier and probably newer and more expensive. One or both might be doing wheelies at the top of the scene. They are in a street or maybe some kind of back alley on their way to get a couple of DVDs.*

TOM. Come on, JJ. What's the big deal? What's going on?

JJ. Don't knock it. We're each getting a DVD out of it.

TOM. Yeah, but how come?

JJ. I'm sworn to secrecy.

TOM. You've been watching too much Austin Powers.

JJ. Is that what you fancy getting out then?

TOM. Austin Powers? No. I'd rather have Johnny English.

JJ. Broad beans and bad jokes. That's what my Mum calls it.

TOM. What does she know?

JJ. Not a lot.

TOM. Shall we go then?

Silence.

TOM *starts to move off.* JJ *hangs back.*

Come on.

JJ. What's a secret thing you wouldn't want anyone else except a best friend to know?

TOM. What is it with you and secrets?

JJ. If I tell you, you tell me?

TOM. Maybe.

JJ. Promise. I won't tell.

TOM. Okay.

JJ. Go on then.

TOM. You first.

JJ. I never slept with Monica. She wouldn't let me. Your turn.

TOM. Do I have to?

JJ. I won't tell.

TOM. I played doctors with Alice's dolls.

Beat.

How about we watch *Lord of the Rings* again?

JJ. *Fellowship* or *Two Towers*?

TOM. *Two Towers*.

JJ. I'd rather see *Matrix*.

Beat

Tom? Can I ask you something?

TOM. Yeah sure.

JJ. Brian's a batty man, isn't he?

TOM. I don't know, is he?

JJ. Yeah. He is.

TOM. So? He's a good teacher.

Beat.

JJ. Would you lie to keep someone out of prison?

TOM. I dunno, JJ. Depends what they'd done I guess.
Depends who they were /

JJ. I'd do it for you, Tom.

TOM. I don't know what you're on about, JJ. I'm not going to
prison.

JJ. I'm talking about supporting your mates when they're
getting grief.

TOM. What've you done?

JJ. I need you to do something for me...

TOM. What?

JJ. I need you to back me up.

TOM. About what?

JJ. About Brian?

TOM. What about him?

JJ. He fancies me.

TOM. What?

JJ. He does. He probably fancies you too. You've got to back me up on this.

TOM. What are you talking about?

JJ. The other day he deliberately had you moved into another room.

TOM. Yeah, because you hadn't done your homework. He wanted you to catch up.

JJ. That was just an excuse. He saw the chance of getting me on my own and he couldn't keep his hands off me.

Pause.

TOM. You're lying…

JJ. You sound like my mum.

TOM. That's bollocks, JJ. It isn't his fault you're crap at maths.

JJ. You're a crap friend.

Beat.

I told my mum.

TOM. Told her what?

Beat.

JJ. I told my mum he touched me up and she believed me.

TOM. Did he?

JJ. He wanted.

TOM. Yeah, but did he? Jesus, JJ, what did you do that for?

JJ. I don't know Tom. I just did. I need you to help me, Tom.

TOM. You want me to say it's true?

JJ. Yeah it is. Say you saw him doing it to me.

TOM. I can't.

JJ. You can.

TOM. I can't.

JJ. Make it up. Just say… he came up close… and touched you up.

TOM. Me? He didn't. No way.

JJ. Go on.

TOM. He didn't.

JJ. I know he didn't. But if you said it. Everyone believes you. If you said it had happened to you, they'd believe me.

Beat.

And then that would be it then, wouldn't it?

TOM. What?

JJ. He'd have to go, wouldn't he?

TOM. Don't see why, it's not true.

JJ. Course he would.

TOM. Why?

JJ. Cos we're underage.

Pause.

TOM. Bloody hell, JJ.

Beat.

What have you got against Brian?

JJ (*interrupts*). What about me? What's everyone got against me? I need you to back me up, Tom. I got Mum to believe me but I don't think Jane will.

TOM. I can't do it. Sorry, JJ.

JJ. You don't have to go into detail. Just say you saw him looking at me and… You thought it was funny when he sent you out. Something. Come on…

TOM. I'm no good at lying.

JJ. It's not difficult.

TOM. I don't want to.

JJ. Please!

TOM. I said I can't do it, JJ.

JJ. You're my best mate for fuck's sake.

TOM. You shitforbrains. You stupid wanker. Look I'd like to help you out but I can't tell lies about a gay man touching you up.

JJ. You've just got to say it. He didn't touch / you up but –

TOM. Jane would never believe me.

JJ. He didn't touch you / but you saw him with me –

TOM. She wouldn't / believe me.

JJ. Just make it up.

TOM. She'd never, ever believe me.

JJ. Why wouldn't she?

TOM. It just wouldn't do any good.

JJ. It would.

TOM. It wouldn't.

JJ. Why?

TOM. Cos Jane's not like that.

JJ. What do you mean?

TOM. She's different about gay men.

JJ. How do you mean?

TOM. She just is.

JJ. I don't understand, Tom.

   Pause.

TOM. Dad's gay for fuck's sake.

   Beat.

JJ. Your dad? Gay? No way.

TOM. He is.

   TOM *starts to leave on his bike.*

   Come on. Let's get *8 Mile.*

JJ. How come he's gay? (*Calling after* TOM.) Wait, Tom. Mum hates rap.

TOM (*offstage*). *Die Another Day* then. Nobody hates Piers Brosnan.

Me, As A Penguin

Tom Wells

☞ **WHO**   Stitch, twenty-two, gay, and Mark, his sister Liz's partner.

☞ **WHERE**   Mark and Liz's sitting room, Hull.

☞ **WHEN**   Present day.

☞ **WHAT HAS JUST HAPPENED**   Stitch, who is gay, has left his small-town home of Withernsea and is staying with his heavily pregnant sister Liz and her partner Mark in Hull, where Stitch plans to explore the gay scene. So far he has only had a rushed and somewhat fumbled encounter with a friend of Mark's called Dave. Dave works with penguins. He helps tour them around to various places, and, because it is half-term, he is now working in the aquarium at the nearby zoo. Stitch has taken his nephew to see the penguins so that it doesn't appear to Mark that he (Stitch) is too keen. But something happens to Stitch when he is at the zoo and without apparent reason he steals a baby penguin and takes it back to the flat where he keeps it hidden in the bath. Mark and Liz find out, but before they can get Dave around to rescue the penguin and put it back, Stitch does a runner with it and it subsequently dies. Meanwhile, Liz goes into labour and gives birth to a baby girl whom they name Emma. Stitch returns to the flat to find Dave waiting to confront him about the dead bird. Although Dave is brash and insensitive to Stitch, Dave suggests that they should have more sex, but Stitch doesn't like the brutality of Dave's approach and turns him down. Then Stitch, who has been taking anti-depressants, attempts to commit suicide. However, he mistakes his bottle of anti-depressants for a similar one he has of kelp. As a result he becomes violently sick and throws up everywhere. In the duologue that follows, Mark, who has returned from the hospital a proud father, helps to clear up the mess.

☞ **WHAT TO CONSIDER**

- This is the last scene of the play, bringing a funny and touching story to a close.

- Back in Withernsea, Stitch works in a craft shop that sells wool, cottons and other haberdashery.

- The sofa that Mark chucks out has been a long-standing bone of contention between him and Liz.

☞ **WHAT STITCH WANTS**

- To apologise.

- To make space for Mark and Liz.

- To return home.

- To feel safe.

- To start over.

☞ **WHAT MARK WANTS**

- For Stitch to confide in him. (Perhaps so that Mark can put his new-found parenting skills to the test.)

- To help Stitch. (Notice how Mark shares his own feelings of vulnerability with Stitch.)

- To start over.

☞ **WHAT THE SCENE IS ABOUT**   Change, realisation, growing up.

STITCH. What's up?

MARK. Nothing, just. (*Sighs.*) I'm shit at clearing up sick. Sort of makes me gag.

STITCH. Oh Mark, you shouldn't be doing that.

MARK. It's fine.

STITCH. No, let me.

   STITCH *takes the cloth, kneels by the sofa and starts wiping the cushions.*

MARK. If you're not up to it.

STITCH. I'm fine.

MARK. Sure?

STITCH. Honestly. Thank you, but.

Pause. MARK *sits on the arm of the sofa and watches* STITCH, *wondering how to approach talking about the night before. The best he can come up with is:*

MARK. So. Been a bit down?

STITCH. Bit down, yeah.

Pause. More cleaning.

MARK. Can't believe you overdosed on kelp.

You'll have such strong nails.

STITCH. Bonus.

Pause. Cleaning.

MARK. Why d'you do it, Stitch?

STITCH. Got the wrong pills.

MARK. No, I meant.

STITCH. Oh. You know. This and that.

Pause.

MARK. Tricky stain?

STITCH. Yeah.

MARK. I couldn't shift it.

STITCH. Have you got any Vanish Mousse?

MARK. Erm. Not that I know of.

STITCH. Flash Spray?

MARK *shakes his head.* STITCH *sniffs the sofa cushion.*

Febreze might help.

MARK. Don't think so.

STITCH. Oust?

MARK. Stitch, you're obviously upset.

STITCH. I just need cleaning products.

MARK (*softening*). Leave it for now, eh? I'll pick something up later, and.

STITCH. No. I want to sort it before I go. Liz might be home tonight, and Emma.

MARK. Don't know why you've got it into your head you have to go.

STITCH *doesn't say anything.*

Liz'll be upset if she's missed you. And you've got to wait and see Emma.

STITCH. I'll see them another time.

MARK. Not the same, though, is it?

STITCH *shrugs.*

Stitch, you'll have to talk to me. I don't understand what's.

STITCH. I had a good think last night. While I was projectile vomiting. And I decided, perhaps the gay scene of Hull isn't for me. It's the vodka, I think. Among other things. Honestly. I looked deep inside myself. And I just found: wool. I'm not a great one for nightclubs, not a party animal. Can't imagine I ever will be. I don't even like sex that much, to be honest. Rather have a good yoghurt. I think the best thing I can hope to do with my life is. Knitting.

MARK. You don't have to –

STITCH. It's alright. I like hanging round with old ladies in experimental cardigans. They're nice. Kind. I fit in. Think they've even twigged about, you know. Always speak very highly of Dale Winton when I'm around, so. Perhaps I'd better just. Do that. For a bit.

Pause.

MARK. Well, I'm not convinced. I thought you wanted to be away from all that.

STITCH. I did. Sort of. Just. I'm not sure I'm. There's days when you feel so buoyant and. Capable. Then something'll just. I dunno. And you're. Overwhelmed this. Sadness. Do you not hear it sometimes? Behind things, everything really, this, I dunno. This sad heart beating.

Pause.

MARK (*dreading the answer*). Have you done it before?

STITCH. Not really.

I thought about it once, but, you know. Nothing came of it.

MARK. When was this?

STITCH. Back home. November-ish. Silly really.

Took myself down to the beach one afternoon. Sat in the shingle, looking for fossils. Didn't find much. Half a devil's toenail. Bit off an ammonite's shell. A tampon. Then I watched the waves for a bit. They've got a rhythm, you know. Sort of: inviting. I thought: I could just keep sitting here, let it wash round me, like arms. No one'd know. Then I thought: actually. Looks a bit cold. Went home and watched *Countdown*. It's not the same without Carol Vorderman but still. Better than. You know.

MARK. Oh, absolutely. Much better, no question. No question about that. (*Pause.*) No question.

STITCH. Alright.

MARK *notices* STITCH *is crying.*

MARK. Oh God, Stitch, just. (*Guiding* STITCH *onto the sofa next to him.*) Sit up here a minute. Hey. (*Puts an arm round him, a bit stiffly.*) Ssh. Hey. Come on. What's up?

STITCH (*quietly, but not crying any more*). I'm in the wet patch.

MARK. Shit, sorry I. Didn't think.

MARK *moves onto the arm,* STITCH *to the dry side of the sofa.*

Sorry.

STITCH. It's fine, I'm sorry. You've just had a baby.

MARK. Not me personally.

STITCH (*getting upset again*). No, but, you don't need all this from some tit who nicked a penguin then tried to top himself.

MARK. Hey.

STITCH. I'm sorry, I –

MARK. Hey. Ssh.

STITCH. I'm so glad you're here.

MARK. Yeah, well, you know. I'm glad you're here.

STITCH. But I mean, I shouldn't be –

MARK. Come on, Stitch. Calm down. Just, tell me what's up.

STITCH (*calming down again*). Oh, I dunno. I'm just so. (*Deep breath.*) Embarrassed.

MARK (*smiles*). Well, there's no need for that for a start. You've not done anything wrong. Listen, if there's one thing I learned when I was working at Ikea: things fall apart.

STITCH *smiles.*

For no reason sometimes. Happens to everyone. Honestly.

STITCH. Yeah?

MARK. Course it does. Before I met your sister, I was in a right state. No job, not eating properly, drinking far too much. We don't really talk about it now, but: I had a mullet. Spent eight months shut up by myself doing a four-foot embroidered portrait of Meat Loaf.

STITCH (*surprised*). That one in the airing cupboard?

MARK *looks more surprised.*

I tried hiding the penguin in there.

MARK (*looking down*). Oh.

STITCH. You made that?

MARK. I'm not proud.

Pause.

STITCH. I didn't know you were into… Meat Loaf and that.

MARK (*smiles*). Not so much these days.

STITCH. But, I mean. It's beautiful.

MARK (*touched*). Oh. Cheers.

STITCH. Bit dark, but.

MARK. It was a dark time for me, if I'm honest. Lonely.

STITCH. What happened?

MARK. Oh, it's. It's boring really. Just, you know. Heartbreak. Lies. All the classics.

STITCH *looks sad.* MARK *sighs.*

Alright. (Deep breath.)

Her name was Lola. She was a showgirl.

STITCH (*smiling*). Not sure I believe that, Mark.

MARK. Fine, her name was Lisa. Worked in Superdrug. Not as funny.

STITCH. You don't have to make it funny.

MARK. I know, just. What you do, isn't it? Take the worst of your life, turn it round. Laugh at it. Cos it can't do any harm, can it? No one ever died of a joke.

STITCH. Suppose.

MARK. Kelp, on the other hand. Lethal.

STITCH (*smiling*). Alright.

MARK. You should try it, though. I mean. Just a thought. Stay here and we'll help.

STITCH. Help laugh at me?

MARK. Yeah.

STITCH. It's a kind offer, Mark.

MARK. Well: I'm all heart.

Eh, are you wavering?

STITCH (*smiles*). Might be.

MARK. Nice one.

I really think it could work. You'd be happy here and that.

Pause. STITCH *thinks about staying here or returning home. He makes his decision, and sticks to it with a new touch of firmness in his voice.*

STITCH. No, it's.

MARK. What?

STITCH. I just think, it's a bit more complicated than –

MARK. You're making excuses now.

STITCH. No. You and Liz and Emma need time together. All that bonding and that. It's important.

MARK. You need to bond too.

STITCH. I will, just. Not yet. State I'm in.

It's so kind of you, honestly, but. I'm ready to go back, really. (*Brave face.*) To Withernsea. It's you they need, Mark.

MARK. Don't say that.

STITCH. It is.

MARK. Doubt I've got it in me.

STITCH. You do, though.

MARK. Stitch, I'm not kidding. I stood there last night watching it all and. I dunno. I mean: I said all the right things and that. Ooh, look at her little fingers, her little toes. Thank God they're not webbed.

STITCH. See?

MARK. This is it, though: there I was, holding her for the first time, heartbeat to heartbeat, the most precious thing I've ever touched. So delicate. Perfect, really. And all I kept thinking in the back of my mind was: I'm still not getting rid of that sofa.

Now this.

They both look at the sofa for a bit.

STITCH. Perhaps a throw might help?

Pause. MARK *sighs, decision made. He borrows the quiet firmness in his voice from* STITCH, *like he's trying it out. It seems to work.*

MARK. No, I.

You wouldn't give us a hand?

STITCH. What d'you mean?

MARK. Get it outside.

STITCH *looks surprised.*

That's the rules. If you go, so does…

STITCH. Oh Mark.

MARK. No, it's good. Fresh start. For Liz and that.

STITCH. Are you sure?

MARK. Think so. Think she'd like that. She was fairly clear.

STITCH (*smiles*). Well. I mean. If you're positive, then.

Pause. MARK *strokes the sofa tenderly.*

MARK. Right. Right then. Let's have it outside.

They carry the sofa offstage.

Mustafa

Naylah Ahmed

☞ **WHO**   Mustafa, thirties, British Asian of Pakistani heritage, and Shabir, early forties, a solicitor, Mustafa's brother. (Out of context these characters could be played younger.)

☞ **WHERE**   The visiting room of a UK prison.

☞ **WHEN**   Present day.

☞ **WHAT HAS JUST HAPPENED**   Mustafa is a devout Muslim. He is serving a prison sentence for the manslaughter of a teenage boy who died during an exorcism. Mustafa has always protested his innocence. His brother Shabir is a solicitor and has been asked by Malik, the dead boy's father, to persuade Mustafa to appeal the sentence. The duologue that follows is Mustafa and Shabir's second meeting in prison.

☞ **WHAT TO CONSIDER**

- The difference between the brothers and their strained relationship. Mustafa adheres to his Pakistani heritage whereas Shabir has become Westernised. Note how disgusted Mustafa is at Shabir's drinking and how Shabir straight away assumes Mustafa's trip to Pakistan has been to do with terrorism.

- The production note: 'Both Mustafa and Shabir came to England as children. They do not have Asian accents. Shabir is well spoken; he pronounces Urdu/Islamic words in an Anglicised way. Mustafa's pronunciation [is] in both Arabic and Urdu for someone with Pakistani heritage; he's not as posh as his brother.'

- 'The visitor' to which Mustafa refers is the djinn or spirit that he maintains killed the boy and is still at large – and at work in the prison.

- '*Ibadat*' is worship, devotion, dedication and commitment.

- '*Tasbih*' are prayer beads.

- '*Hafiz*' is one who has committed the Qur'an (Islamic religious text, more usually spelled 'Koran') to heart and is able to recite it from memory.

- 'Asr' is the third of the five daily prayers.
- Words in [square brackets] are there to indicate intention, and not to be spoken.

☞ WHAT MUSTAFA WANTS

- To explain to Shabir exactly what happened and for Shabir to believe him.
- His brother's love.
- Forgiveness. (Despite the fact that he knows he did not kill the boy, Mustafa still feels guilty.)

☞ WHAT SHABIR WANTS

- To help his brother. (To what extent is this born out of a sense of family duty? Or is he seeking to reconnect with Mustafa on a more intimate and emotional level?)
- Respect from Mustafa. (Note how he feels dismissed and disapproved of by his younger brother.)

☞ WHAT THE SCENE IS ABOUT   Family, sibling rivalry, religion, the clash of cultures, the supernatural.

SHABIR. Okay, so we got off on the wrong foot the other day. I'm sorry if it was anything I said. I appreciate it can't be easy in here… it must be… Anyway, I'm sorry it's taken longer than I said to come back.

…

Mustafa?

MUSTAFA. How's your wife?

SHABIR. She's… good, she's fine, thanks, thanks for asking.

…

Look, this is all nice, you and me and this. But, bottom line, it isn't going to help us get you out of here.

MUSTAFA. I don't think they let murderers go that easy, Shabir.

SHABIR. Manslaughter. You've been convicted and sentenced for manslaughter with diminished responsibility. Unless you're telling me something new?

MUSTAFA. A boy died. Whatever they call it, whatever terms you use…

SHABIR. These aren't terms, Mustafa, it's the law. Manslaughter with diminished responsibility – fourteen years – do you know what that means?

…

You look worse than last time. Have you slept?

MUSTAFA. No. Had a… visitor.

SHABIR. Who? Malik?

MUSTAFA. No. Forget it. Look, I never intended to get you mixed up in this.

SHABIR. Well, that's the thing about family, isn't it; intend it, don't intend, it makes no difference.

MUSTAFA. Why are you here?

SHABIR. What? I told you, Malik asked me –

MUSTAFA. I mean, why did you come. When you found out?

SHABIR. Isn't it obvious?

…

MUSTAFA. They giving you a hard time at work?

SHABIR. Look, we need to –

MUSTAFA. Are they?

SHABIR. I'm a partner. While you were away, I… I'm a partner at the firm now.

MUSTAFA. Congratulations.

SHABIR. One with a brother who's been convicted of killing some kid during an exorcism. Congratulations are… pointless.

MUSTAFA. That's why you're here.

SHABIR. What difference does it make?

MUSTAFA. A lot. To me.

SHABIR. Wish you'd have stayed in Pakistan. Mind you, I don't know what you were up to over there.

MUSTAFA. Training, I guess.

SHABIR. Oh, for heaven's sake – you weren't... Please don't tell me you were up some mountain with a Kalashnikov!

MUSTAFA. Ibadat – I was learning under Amil Zahid Hus[sain] –

SHABIR. Oh, that would be right. I should have known, minute you hit the ground I bet you were off in some cave meditating with nothing but your tasbih and a –

MUSTAFA. Don't do this.

SHABIR. Why? A boy is dead, just like you said.

MUSTAFA. Yes.

SHABIR. There are people out there who are mourning your sentence, thinking you *saved* this boy from some... some...

MUSTAFA. Djinn. You can't even say it... And what do the others think? Some people think I'm a hero, and the others...?

SHABIR. Think you're a crazed Mullah who killed a boy who may have suffered from a mental disorder.

MUSTAFA *gets up and kicks back his chair.* SHABIR *nods through the glass to an unseen officer, indicating everything is okay.*

MUSTAFA. If you think that then you really shouldn't be [here] –

SHABIR. That's not what I said.

MUSTAFA. But it's what you're thinking.

SHABIR. Is it?

...

MUSTAFA (*pointing*). There.

SHABIR (*looking down at his body*). What?

MUSTAFA. That vein on your neck. It's twitching. Always twitches when you're nervous.

SHABIR. I'm not nerv[ous] –

MUSTAFA. Yeah you are. You're trying to convince me to appeal when you don't believe I should.

SHABIR. What I am doing is acting as your legal representative.

MUSTAFA. How much did you have to drink before you came here?

SHABIR. What?

MUSTAFA. How much – surely, as your client, I deserve to know?

...

Don't look now, but it's twitching.

SHABIR. Fuck you.

...

MUSTAFA. Here's the thing, Shabir. Some people think I'm a hero and some people think I'm a murderer. But they're all out there living their lives and I'm in here. Alone. And there's nothing you can do about it.

SHABIR. I can get a sentence reduction. I know I can.

...

SHABIR *grabs his bag and empties some files on to the table.*

Tell me what happened.

MUSTAFA. You've read the files.

SHABIR. I want to know from you first.

MUSTAFA. I can't do this...

SHABIR. Everything. Start with the boy.

This is it, make or break.

SHABIR *gestures for* MUSTAFA *to sit. He does so. This isn't going to be easy for him, but he sits.*

MUSTAFA. He wasn't just some kid. You know him. Kamran. I taught him Qur'an from maybe four, five years old.

SHABIR. I remember.

MUSTAFA. He wanted to be a Hafiz but his mum wasn't up for it.

SHABIR. Because of you?

MUSTAFA. Because it meant his secular education would take a back seat and she didn't want that. Didn't want the Qur'an to take up space in his mind that GCSE Biology might need… I stopped teaching him when he was about eight, he was a quick learner, finished the Qur'an about three times while he was with me. But I still saw him around after that, saw his dad.

SHABIR. Malik.

MUSTAFA. Yeah. Lived close by for years, saw them all the time…

SHABIR. So when this… happened, he was seventeen?

MUSTAFA. Yes. I went to Pakistan, was there for a year, maybe more. When I got back, I didn't see Malik or Kamran. Heard people talking about them, though, saying the boy had lost weight, lost his hair… They said he was possessed.

SHABIR. So you went to see him?

MUSTAFA. No, I prayed for him. Then one day, Malik comes to my door. He was in a state. He wanted me to come and see his son – he'd only just heard I was back.

SHABIR. And…?

MUSTAFA. He wasn't the boy I remembered. Was older, of course, but smaller – least, it seemed like it. Weak, thin, pulled half his hair out – bitten the inside of his cheeks out…

SHABIR. Had they been to a doctor?

MUSTAFA. Didn't ask.

SHABIR. But –

MUSTAFA. I'm not a physician – that's not why I was there.
He'd been like that for over a year apparently. Whole
family was… sad, burdened. House was black with smoke
in places. They hadn't bothered to fix it, paint it.

SHABIR. Smoke?

MUSTAFA. Malik said if they upset him – if he got angry –
fires would just start up. Kitchen, corner of the living room
– telly exploded.

SHABIR. So you agreed to an exorcism?

MUSTAFA. No. I saw the boy, sat with him. We prayed
together. Seemed to be doing okay, even ate with him, to
encourage him, and he managed to get some food in and
some sleep. Then one day I'm sitting on the settee with
Malik and his daughter and Kamran gets angry. Starts
yelling, kicking off.

SHABIR. Kicking off?

MUSTAFA. Screaming, he was in a rage – his voice wasn't
his own, it was…

SHABIR. There are mental conditions that –

MUSTAFA. He grabbed one foot of the settee and lifts it
right up – with us three still on it. Three, maybe four feet
in the air. Slams it down. His sister goes flying, Malik starts
having an asthma attack…

SHABIR *scribbles a note down.*

Mental conditions exist, course they do, voices can change,
people self-harm… But no one lights a fire in a room
they're not in without so much as a match… no one lifts
three people and a settee four foot into the air one-handed
cos of some mental disorder.

SHABIR. But with all the chaos and Malik's asthma – the
family were already so distressed that…

MUSTAFA. They imagined it? That we all hallucinated
together?

SHABIR. I'm not [saying that] –

MUSTAFA. Yes you are. I don't know what it is about the truth when it gets a bit difficult, out of the norm. Passes from me to you and it becomes... a tale. A comic book – bit of entertainment.

SHABIR. I'm trying to understand.

MUSTAFA. So if you don't understand then it's not true? It didn't happen?

SHABIR. This is no time for philosophising, Mustafa. You went into a room with a perfectly healthy seventeen-year-old and when you came out he was dead.

MUSTAFA. Perfectly healthy? Have you been listening to anything I've –

SHABIR. He was alive. He was alive and then he wasn't. You were in there with him. You were the only one in there with him.

MUSTAFA. You're trying to make sense out of it. Cold, British, legal sense. Your face, looks just like the barrister and the jury and the judge. You should go.

SHABIR. Mustafa –

MUSTAFA. It's time for Asr.

SHABIR. See, this is what you do – always – you walk away.

MUSTAFA. I'm not going anywhere. Not for a long time.

SHABIR. And I want to change that. But I just don't see how –

MUSTAFA. You don't have to see, you have to believe.

SHABIR. You pleaded not guilty.

MUSTAFA. I'm in prison because a boy died. I pleaded not guilty because I didn't take his life. But he died, and I can't change that.

MUSTAFA *stands.* SHABIR *begins, reluctantly, to gather his things together. As* MUSTAFA *passes to get to the door,* SHABIR *grabs his hand.*

SHABIR. I've heard – about the things that have been going on with you here. The way the officers talk… can't imagine what the prisoners are saying.

MUSTAFA. Did you tell them you're my brother?

SHABIR. It's not the way to go if you want to get out early – you can't keep –

MUSTAFA. I didn't do those things. Any of them.

SHABIR. Enough! Haven't you had enough? What do you expect me to say to that? You smashed a tray in some guy's face – some young, tough, white criminal's face – in here – and you expect things to go smoothly?

MUSTAFA. He did it to himself.

SHABIR. Oh, come on, if you think selling ghost stories to this lot will make your time easier, you're wrong! You scalded some other guy in the showers.

MUSTAFA. The temperature changed – he was goading me and the water got hotter and hotter and he just stood there. You think I control the water temperature in the prison showers?

SHABIR. Then who, Mustafa – if not you, then who?

MUSTAFA. The djinn –

SHABIR. Oh, God help me…

MUSTAFA. – that left the boy is here.

SHABIR. Listen to yourself –

MUSTAFA. I see it, I hear it. Sometimes in the officers. Sometimes in the prisoners. It does things.

SHABIR. This is childish – this is crazy…

MUSTAFA. It's also true. Believe, don't believe, doesn't make it any less true. The world doesn't disappear if you close your eyes to it, Shabir.

SHABIR. Thanks, Yoda. Any more pearls of wisdom?

MUSTAFA *smiles.*

What could possibly be amusing right now?

MUSTAFA. We watched that together, Yoda, Han Solo, Luke…

SHABIR. Yes.

MUSTAFA. I broke your Millennium Falcon – remember?

…

SHABIR. Malik says he wants to visit. It'll look good – victim's father coming to see you – both here and in court. You should see him.

MUSTAFA *shakes his head.*

MUSTAFA. The *Star Wars Trilogy* at the Odeon in town – all three films back to back. That was a good day.

SHABIR. It was a good day. Not like this.

MUSTAFA. I didn't want you to get mixed up in this. That's why I didn't call.

SHABIR. I'll look over the paperwork tonight.

End of scene.

My Night with Reg
Kevin Elyot

☞ **WHO**   John, late thirties, upper-middle class, gay, handsome, and Guy, late thirties, middle-class, gay, not obviously good-looking.

☞ **WHERE**   The sitting room of Guy's flat. London.

☞ **WHEN**   1980s.

☞ **WHAT HAS JUST HAPPENED**   Set in the 1980s, the play tells the story of a group of gay men. Three of them – John, Guy and Daniel – are friends from university. For nine years Guy and John were out of touch, but at the start of the play all three are reunited when Guy throws a housewarming supper. Guy has always harboured a deep love for John; when they were students Guy thought that John might have felt the same. He has never told John about his feelings towards him, despite being goaded by Daniel to do so. Daniel's partner is Reg (although he never appears in the play). Unbeknownst to Daniel, and as revealed in the duologue that follows, Reg has been having an affair with John. The play then moves forward a couple of years. Reg has died of AIDS, and Guy is now hosting the wake after the funeral. In the scene directly before this duologue, Guy has told Eric (a young, good-looking gay man who used to be Guy's painter/decorator) about his feelings towards John. Eric tells Guy that he should tell John and goes to fetch him.

☞ **WHAT TO CONSIDER**

- Being gay in London in the 1980s. If you were 'out' it was a time of increased confidence, and there were a number of openly gay clubs and pubs where you could meet and party.

- This same abandonment, however, led to panic as increasing numbers of gay men died of AIDS following unprotected sex with one another.

- Because of his clandestine affair with Reg, John is terrified that he too will die.

- In a previous scene Guy confesses that the only time he had unprotected sex was on holiday during a one-night stand. He too is scared of dying of an AIDS-related illness. (Read the play to find out what happens to Guy.)

- It was Guy who stole John's jockstrap. He still has it.

- After Reg's funeral we find out that Reg has slept with all of the men in the play apart from Guy. John in the meantime is unaware of this, although Guy knows full well the extent of Reg's promiscuity.

- The impact of Reg's death on Guy. It reminds him that life is short and is in many ways the spur that allows him to speak to John. After all, what has he got to lose?

- When John says, 'he's left me nothing you know', he is talking about Reg.

☞ WHAT JOHN WANTS

- To reassure Guy that he is desirable.

- To encourage him to make a move on Eric.

- To talk about Reg.

- Reassurance that he is not a bad person.

- Comfort in the face of death.

☞ WHAT GUY WANTS

- To tell of his love for John and for John to reciprocate. (It has taken him fifteen years to pluck up the courage to tell John how he feels.)

- To admonish John despite being in love with him. (Note how quickly John needs to talk about Reg, leaving Guy feeling foolish and jealous.)

☞ WHAT THE SCENE IS ABOUT   Unfulfilled desire, loss, love, abandonment, fear of mortality.

☞ NB   This play offers a number of other duologues from which to choose.

JOHN. Eric said you wanted a word.

GUY. Did he? Are you alright?

JOHN. Yeah.

He lights a cigarette.

He's cute.

GUY. Yes. Yes, he is.

JOHN. So what did you want?

GUY. Nothing really.

JOHN. Up to my eyes in it, aren't I?

Beat.

GUY. If you want a bit of company, if you ever want to stay, you know you're welcome.

JOHN. Yeah. Thanks. Do you know, I've never understood why someone hasn't snapped you up?

GUY. Really?

JOHN. Yes. I mean, you're such a nice guy, you're so… It's not fair, is it? Still, it'll happen one day, I'm sure. Do you see much of him?

GUY. Who?

JOHN. Eric.

GUY. From time to time. Mainly at the pub.

JOHN. What about him?

GUY. What do you mean?

JOHN. Have you ever thought about giving Eric a go?

GUY. As you say, he's… cute, but –

JOHN. He can only say no and he likes you, doesn't he?

GUY. I think so, but 'like' isn't the issue.

Beat.

The way some of these young ones look at me, or not, as the case may be! I know I'm nearly forty, but my dick hasn't dropped off.

Beat.

But yes, he's cute. You're right.

JOHN. You should tell him.

GUY. Yes, maybe I should.

JOHN. Anyway, you deserve someone.

GUY. John?

JOHN. Yes?

Beat.

GUY. You remember *The Bacchae*?

JOHN. Mm?

GUY. And the last-night party, when we were up in the flies?

JOHN. Up in the flies... Yes! I remember! That little
     scumbag playing – whatever it was –

GUY. Pentheus.

JOHN. That's it! He chucked his ring, didn't he?

GUY. Yes, but I meant before that.

JOHN. Before he threw up?

GUY. Before he arrived.

JOHN. Right.

Beat.

GUY. We were having a bit of a chat.

JOHN. Uh-huh.

GUY. We were... well, you said something –

JOHN. Do you know, some bastard nicked my jockstrap?

GUY. Did they?

JOHN. Yes! Not that I wanted it, but... sorry, what were you
     saying?

GUY. Up in the flies, we were having a chat and a bottle of
     wine and you were telling me about yourself.

JOHN. What did I say?

GUY. Lots of things.

JOHN. Was I pissed?

GUY. Not particularly. And after a while, you said something to me that I thought meant that you might want to…

JOHN. What?

GUY. That I thought meant you might…

Beat.

Do you remember?

JOHN. I remember Pentheus throwing up.

Beat.

GUY. He was a bit of a pain, wasn't he?

JOHN. Yeah.

Beat.

He's left me nothing, you know.

Beat.

GUY. Well, it'd have been a bit difficult, wouldn't it? Daniel not knowing and everything.

JOHN. But I can't help wondering. I haven't loved anyone before. He knocked me for six. The first time in my life when I felt I wasn't in control. Do you think he loved me?

GUY. I wouldn't know. I hardly ever saw you together and he never talked about it because he didn't know I knew.

JOHN. Did you like him?

GUY. Yes.

JOHN. Really?

GUY. Yes. Well, I suppose my opinion of him went down a bit after you'd told me about the two of you.

JOHN. Did your opinion of me go down a bit?

GUY. No.

JOHN. Why not? We were both shitting on Daniel.

Beat.

GUY. To be honest, I did think you should've told him, but you're going to, aren't you?

JOHN. It's over now. Why disillusion him?

GUY. But in one sense, it's not over, is it? Dan'll carry on talking about him and we'll carry on lying.

JOHN. That's better than spoiling it for him. He was happy with Reg. So was I. Why fuck it up?

GUY. Maybe this isn't the best time to talk about it. You've had the most awful day –

JOHN. And if I do tell him – and I'm not saying I never will – how much should I tell him? All of it? Part of it? Once I'd started, where would I stop?

GUY. But I can't help feeling that Reg was having his cake and eating it.

JOHN. What's it matter?

GUY. Quite a few cakes, by all accounts.

Beat.

JOHN. What?

GUY. Well… he wasn't exactly a saint, was he?

JOHN. What do you mean?

GUY. I'm not telling you anything new.

JOHN. What are you telling me?

GUY. Nothing.

JOHN. Guy!

GUY. I suppose all I'm saying is that if he could do that to Daniel, why couldn't he do it to you?

JOHN. He was having an affair?

GUY. No, no! I'm just telling you what you already know.

JOHN. And what's that?

GUY. That fidelity wasn't exactly his strong point.

JOHN. Wasn't it?

GUY. For Christ's sake, John, the very fact that he had an affair with you!

JOHN. Who else?

GUY. I don't know.

JOHN. Who?

GUY. No one!

JOHN pours a Scotch.

I'm sorry. It's not my place…

He gulps it down.

I just didn't like the way he treated you – both of you. That's all.

JOHN pours another.

You just can't carry on like that.

He gulps it down.

This is the wrong time. We really shouldn't be talking about it.

JOHN. Even if he did… a bit on the side… what's it matter? It doesn't take anything away… What the fuck's it matter?

GUY. But it does matter! What the hell was he playing at? It was so irresponsible. Even the vicar told me what a good fuck he was outside the crematorium! God, I'm sorry. I'm sorry. I didn't mean to say that. I'm sorry. It's because I'm worried about you, about Daniel and the lot of you. I'm sorry. I really didn't mean to.

JOHN. One minute! I mean, what do you say to someone when you know it's the last time?

GUY. John –

JOHN. What do you say? I leant over, smelt his hair, kissed his cheek, managed to say, 'I love you' and before he could say anything, Daniel had come back. He told me hundreds of times he loved me, but the one time that would've mattered was the last and Daniel came back to the bedside. Maybe he didn't in the end. When you're dying, maybe things fall into place and Dan was the only person who counted –

GUY. John –

JOHN. And now I'll never know.

Beat.

You're probably thinking, 'I could have told you so.' But those few years – it could've been a night and it'd have been worth it.

Beat.

I'm frightened.

GUY. Yes.

Beat. He touches JOHN's arm. JOHN *doesn't respond.*

Nineteen Ninety-Two*

Lisa McGee

☞ **WHO**   Two Northern Irish brothers. David, twenty-seven, and John Paul, twenty-three.

☞ **WHERE**   'The middle of nowhere.' (Somewhere near Liverpool in the living room of a run-down country house.)

☞ **WHEN**   2009.

☞ **WHAT HAS JUST HAPPENED**   The following duologue is a short two-hander and a complete play in itself.

☞ **WHAT TO CONSIDER**

- The play's black humour. What starts out as a bit of ribaldry between brothers takes on an altogether different turn as we realise what, or rather who, is in the box.

- The violent and shocking nature of the original crime. There is something particularly disturbing about a child who kills another child and, because it seems to go against nature, we are even more disturbed when the murderer is female. It is a subject that Lisa McGee further explores in her play *Girls and Dolls*.

- The possibility that the brothers have the wrong girl.

☞ **WHAT DAVID WANTS**

- For John Paul to remain calm and focused.

- Revenge.

☞ **WHAT JOHN PAUL WANTS**

- Reassurance that they have the right girl and are doing the right thing

- To join with David in torturing the girl. (He does this verbally if not physically.)

- To prove his toughness.

---

* Published in the volume *Irish Shorts*

- Forgiveness. (Note how much more unsure he is than his older brother.)

☞ **WHAT THE SCENE IS ABOUT**   Revenge, righting the wrongs of the past, violence breeding violence.

☞ **NB**   This volume offers a number of other duologues from which to choose.

DAVID *sits at a cheap patio table with a newspaper spread out in front of him. He struggles with a crossword puzzle. The only item in decent condition, a fairly large wooden strongbox, sits at the opposite end of the room.* JOHN PAUL *sits on the box examining his bruised face in a shaving mirror. His shirt is stained with his own blood. The floor is covered with pieces of screwed-up newspapers. In the centre of the room hangs a noose with a stack of books directly underneath it.*

DAVID (*re: crossword*). Something – something – something – E – something – something – S?

JOHN PAUL (*examining his face, wincing in pain*). Ah... it's every time I open my mouth... I can... ah... I can hear a crack... I can hear like a cracking sound.... .

DAVID (*re: crossword*). 'This Greek daughter may oppose your purpose?'

JOHN PAUL (*opens his mouth*). Can you hear that? Can you? It's like a cracking sound.

DAVID. Greek daughter?

JOHN PAUL. Look at the state of me...

DAVID. Something – something – something...

JOHN PAUL. Look at the fucking state of me.

DAVID. E – something – something – S?

JOHN PAUL. Do you hear me?

DAVID. Something – something – something – E...

JOHN PAUL. Shut up.

DAVID *looks up from his crossword.*

DAVID. Or what?

JOHN PAUL. Or I – something – will – something – knock your fuck in – something.

DAVID. What's your problem?

JOHN PAUL. My face looks like I'm wearing it inside out. That's my problem.

DAVID. It was an accident.

JOHN PAUL. You should think about where your fist might land the next time you throw it.

DAVID. You got in my way… it was an accident… I hardly meant to hit you. What, you think I meant to hit you?

JOHN PAUL. I don't care if you meant to do it. The fact is, you did it. It's done.

DAVID. And all the crying in the world won't undo it so dry your eyes.

JOHN PAUL. You tore skin…

DAVID. No I did not…

JOHN PAUL. You did… look… you tore fucking skin – although to be fair that gyppo sovereign ring you insist on wearing did most of the damage .

DAVID. It's not a sovereign ring.

JOHN PAUL. It's still bleeding.

DAVID. It's a signature ring…

JOHN PAUL. And there's like… there's like a dent…

DAVID. It's called a signature ring…

JOHN PAUL. There… beneath my eye… you could have had my fucking eye out.

DAVID. Jesus Christ, how many times I didn't do it on purpose.

JOHN PAUL *approaches* DAVID.

JOHN PAUL. Feel it go…

DAVID. I will not…

JOHN PAUL. Go on… feel.

DAVID. I will not feel. Fuck off.

DAVID *returns to his crossword.*

JOHN PAUL. It's probably gonna scar you know…

DAVID. Probably.

JOHN PAUL (*shocked*). You think it's gonna scar! Jesus Christ!

DAVID. Relax, John Paul, I've done you a favour. It could only be an improvement.

JOHN PAUL. Everyone says I look just like you, David.

DAVID. Aye… after a stroke maybe.

JOHN PAUL. Fuck off, fuckwit.

DAVID. 'Fuck off, fuckwit'? I wish I had such an extensive vocabulary… this crossword would be a piece of piss…

JOHN PAUL. Will you just admit defeat and give up…

DAVID. That's the spirit.

JOHN PAUL. You're not gonna finish it, you've never finished one.

DAVID. That's not true…

JOHN PAUL. You're the same with them sudoku things… you just frustrate yourself… why do you even try?

DAVID. The same reason you continue to talk to women I imagine… there's a slight chance I might actually get somewhere.

JOHN PAUL (*dry*). That's good. That's brilliant…

DAVID. Do you know what though? You're right.

DAVID *turns the paper over.*

This is pointless.

DAVID *starts to read the paper.* JOHN PAUL *looks around the room. He goes to the window. He stares out.*

JOHN PAUL. The English countryside is a lot duller than the Irish countryside isn't it?

DAVID. Definitely. Do you know why?

JOHN PAUL. Is it something to do with rain?

DAVID. Partly, but mostly it's because you're a biased bastard.

JOHN PAUL *laughs slightly.*

JOHN PAUL. Yeah maybe. (*Beat.*) How did you come across this place anyway?

DAVID. That… that weekend I… that weekend I came over with the boys for Mickey's stag…

JOHN PAUL. Yeah…

DAVID. Well, after it happened… you know after I saw…

JOHN PAUL. After you saw her?

DAVID. Well, my head was just… you know…

JOHN PAUL (*sympathetic*). Of course it was.

DAVID. I needed to think so I got in the car Mickey hired and I just drove. I didn't even tell the lads I was going. I just got in the car and drove… suddenly I'm out here… looking at this place…

JOHN PAUL. I still can't believe you bought it.

DAVID. It had only been on the market for a matter of days you know. This old widower… he'd lived here for over fifty years… then the week before I pull up outside… he decides to drop. Fate.

JOHN PAUL. Fate?

DAVID. Fate.

JOHN PAUL. So what'll you do with it after… when it's… (*Beat.*) What'll you do when it's over, you know when it's finished… when it's done?

DAVID. Wait awhile then sell it I suppose.

JOHN PAUL. You will be waiting awhile.

DAVID. I don't give a shit.

JOHN PAUL. Like it's the middle of fucking nowhere...

DAVID. It's half an hour from Liverpool, JP.

JOHN PAUL. I can't believe you actually bought it.

DAVID (*annoyed*). We needed somewhere didn't we?

JOHN PAUL (*quietly*). Yeah.

DAVID. We couldn't exactly do this in a hotel room could we?

JOHN PAUL. No.

DAVID. We needed somewhere private.

A silence. The mood is tense.

JOHN PAUL (*lighter*). Well, it is that... It's private alright. Nobody or nothing around... not as much as a fucking sheep. (*Shudders.*) Thank Christ.

DAVID. I can't believe you're still afraid of sheep.

JOHN PAUL. Creepy wee fuckers.

DAVID. You should get hypnotherapy, John Paul...

JOHN PAUL. That's a pile of balls...

DAVID. It's not. Remember Mary Morgan?

JOHN PAUL. Mary from Derry?

DAVID. Mary from Derry aye. She was scared shitless of clowns. She went and got hypnotised, she's totally fine now... they don't bother her.

JOHN PAUL. Naw... I don't need to. Sure I'm never even around sheep...

DAVID. Well, Mary's not out drinking with Coco and Krusty every Friday night either, but it's an irrational fear. It should be dealt with.

JOHN PAUL. Well, I've coped so far.

DAVID *returns to his paper.*

A silence.

I'd like to have done this at home.

DAVID. Well, that's not possible.

JOHN PAUL. It would've been better at home.

DAVID. John Paul… come on…

JOHN PAUL. This is… I didn't want to say anything. I've been trying not to say anything but… it's playing on my nerves a bit now.

DAVID. I know. You're alright though. It's alright.

JOHN PAUL. It's this… it's just this waiting… it's just this hanging about…

DAVID. I'll make us a cup of tea…

JOHN PAUL. Good… yeah… I think I'm about ready for my seventy-fifth cup of tea …

DAVID. What do you want me to do?

JOHN PAUL. I don't know make coffee… or hot chocolate or something… mix it up a bit… keep me on my toes.

DAVID. We don't have any hot chocolate…

JOHN PAUL. Jesus, my head's wrecked.

DAVID. And mine isn't?

JOHN PAUL. I know. I'm sorry. It's the waiting. I can't cope with it… the waiting.

DAVID *takes a bottle of water and fills the kettle on the table with it. He switches it on. He rattles around in a plastic bag.*

DAVID. Do you want a Hobnob?

JOHN PAUL. What?

DAVID. A Hobnob?

JOHN PAUL. I heard you. Where the fuck did you pull the Hobnobs from?

DAVID. I got them in that garage we stopped at…

JOHN PAUL. And why are they only surfacing now?

DAVID. I forgot about them…

JOHN PAUL. Forgot about them my hole… you were keeping them shy.

DAVID. I wasn't keeping them shy… if I was keeping them shy I wouldn't ask you if you wanted one.

JOHN PAUL. You're as fly as fuck.

DAVID. All I did was offer you a biscuit.

JOHN PAUL. Are they caramel or regular…

DAVID. Regular.

JOHN PAUL. Aye alright then.

The kettle boils. DAVID *begins to make the tea.*

Nothing changes. You would always hoard your sweets when we were weans.

DAVID. I was not hoarding the Hobnobs.

DAVID *finishes making the tea. He brings a cup to* JOHN PAUL. *He stops before reaching him, freezes and stares out the window.*

JOHN PAUL. Well, are you gonna give me it or warm your hands with it?

DAVID. I'm gonna fuck it round you…

JOHN PAUL. What?

DAVID. Which part of 'park the car around the back' confused you exactly?

JOHN PAUL. It's fine.

DAVID. It's not fine, John Paul… anybody could drive past… anybody could see…

JOHN PAUL. Nobody's gonna drive past. We might as well be up a mountain in a cave…

DAVID. Jesus but you're useless. We can't draw attention to us… to this. We can't draw attention to it.

DAVID *hands* JOHN PAUL *his tea.*

Here. I'll do it myself.

DAVID *lifts a set of car keys from the table. He walks towards the door.*

Useless fucking bastard.

DAVID *exits.* JOHN PAUL *now alone. Sips his tea. After a few moments a faint knocking sound can be heard, it's coming from inside the box.* JOHN PAUL *looks at the box. He puts his tea down and stares at it. After a few moments more* DAVID *re-enters.* DAVID *stares at* JOHN PAUL *who is completed fixated on the box.*

What is it?

JOHN PAUL. Knocking…

DAVID (*re: box*). From in there?

JOHN PAUL. Yeah.

They listen. Silence.

DAVID *returns to his chair at the patio table. He opens the paper again.*

DAVID. Open it up and check if you want.

JOHN PAUL. What, now?

DAVID. If you want?

JOHN PAUL. You don't want to?

DAVID. Are you afraid?

JOHN PAUL. Piss off.

DAVID. Open it then. Check.

DAVID *reads his paper.* JOHN PAUL *cautiously opens the strongbox and stares inside. A few moments of silence pass.*

Well… has she come round?

JOHN PAUL. I dunno.

DAVID. What do you mean you don't know? Is she awake?

JOHN PAUL. I dunno.

DAVID. Are her eyes open?

JOHN PAUL. I can't tell… we… David, we…

DAVID. What?

JOHN PAUL. I think we fucked her face up pretty bad…

DAVID *takes a sip of his tea, he turns a page of his paper.*

It's all swollen out… her head's huge now…

DAVID. She's not already dead is she?

JOHN PAUL. No she's breathing.

DAVID. Good.

JOHN PAUL. Let's just do it…

DAVID. No.

JOHN PAUL. Please… come on… please…

DAVID. I'm not finished.

JOHN PAUL. Let's just do it. Let's douse the bitch in petrol and spark her up.

DAVID. I'm not finished with her yet.

JOHN PAUL *starts to close the box but suddenly notices something else…*

JOHN PAUL. Did you… did you cut her hair off?

DAVID. Does that milk taste funny to you?

JOHN PAUL. Did you cut off her hair?

DAVID. I think it's out of date…

JOHN PAUL. You shouldn't have done that. Not without me. Why did you cut her hair off, David?

DAVID (*matter of fact*). She cut off his hair, do you remember?

JOHN PAUL. No.

DAVID. She did. He had long hair… do you remember?

JOHN PAUL. Yeah…

DAVID. Too long for a boy… he looked like a girl… do you remember? It embarrassed me back then. I would say to Mammy, 'He looks like a wee girl, people are gonna think he's a wee girl.' Do you remember?

JOHN PAUL. I remember. I remember his hair. I don't remember that she cut it off.

DAVID. She did.

JOHN PAUL. I don't remember ever hearing that.

DAVID. They maybe never told you because you were that bit younger, but she cut off his hair. Before she did it she cut off his fucking hair...

JOHN PAUL. I think... I'd like this to be over already. I'd like for us to do this now.

DAVID. I'm not finished with her yet. When I'm finished with her we won't have to do anything. When I'm finished with her she'll walk over to that rope herself, put it round her own neck and swing the way she should have done a long time ago. You'll see. Trust me.

JOHN PAUL *stares in the box again.* DAVID *returns to his paper.*

Close it again.

JOHN PAUL. I can't believe I'm this close to her... finally.

DAVID. I would fantasise about seeing her, and when I did I always imagined it would happen in some faraway place, some remote town in New Zealand or Australia... when really she was just across the water, she was in here in Liverpool. Six years in a detention centre...

JOHN PAUL (*correcting*). Six years in a fucking holiday camp.

DAVID. Six years then they slap her on the wrists... they say 'be a good girl... don't do it again'... and they let her start a new life within spitting distance of his fucking family...

JOHN PAUL. It's unbelievable.

DAVID. If it wasn't for that weekend we'd be none the wiser. The funny thing is I didn't want to go on Mickey's stag at all. I tried to cancel but the boys were having none of it. I wasn't really in the mood for it... or for them. I only walked into that bookshop to get away for them for five fucking minutes. (*Beat.*) And there she was... I knew right away... I mean she'd changed. I mean of course she'd changed, she was twelve then... She was only twelve then.

JOHN PAUL. And he was only three.

DAVID. Nineteen ninety-two… a long time ago I suppose… but I still fucking knew… I probably know her face better than she does, I was so scared I'd forget. I would study her photograph, I would stare at those newspaper cuttings until my vision blurred, do you remember?

JOHN PAUL. I do.

DAVID. Every feature, every flaw, every freckle… I knew. She hadn't a clue who I was. I bought this book from her… Ruth Rendell or P.D. James or… I don't know some fucking thing. I chucked it as soon as I got out of there. When I went to the counter with it I didn't speak. I was careful not to. I was afraid she might guess somehow… my accent or something, she's lost hers…

JOHN PAUL. I know.

DAVID. Did you hear her speak?

JOHN PAUL. She cried out. She cried out for help… 'it wasn't me' she kept saying.

DAVID. She doesn't sound like she was ever Irish. That day in the shop she said… 'It's really good that one.' She was talking about the book… and she smiled at me… like she had the right to talk… like she had the right to smile… and when she gave me my change her hand touched mine and I had to… I had to get out of there quickly… I had to practically run out of there because I knew I was going to vomit and I did… I did. All over pavement… all over the pavement and all over myself.

JOHN PAUL. 'It wasn't me… It was somebody else.'

DAVID. I stayed in here for a week you know?

JOHN PAUL. 'That was somebody else.' She kept saying.

DAVID. I stayed in Liverpool. I stayed for a week after that. I watched her for a week before I told you. I watched her go to work… I watched her go for lunch… I followed her home… a whole week… and her life it's just… it seems normal… ordinary… like she's walking about pretending to be one of us…

JOHN PAUL. When she was calling out like... I started to doubt you, David. But then I realised what she meant... she meant that she wasn't that person any more, that she was different, that she was somebody else. (*Speaks into the box.*) It wasn't just him you know. That day you saw him in the park. That day he put his little trusting hand in yours. That day you led him away. Well, you didn't just take him... you took our mother, you took our poor fucking father, you ruined them, you ruined us. You don't get to be somebody else. You fucking animal. You evil fucking animal.

DAVID. Close it over.

JOHN PAUL *closes the box and sits on it. He picks up his tea again.*

Do you know what I always think about? When we were young... when he was alive and the three of us were children, Ma and Da would warn us about strangers, 'don't takes sweets, don't get into cars'... but the strangers were always men... bad men... we were all so busy watching out for bad men we forgot about bad women... we either forgot or we thought they didn't exist.

DAVID *turns back to his crossword again.* JOHN PAUL *takes a sip of his tea.*

JOHN PAUL. This is freezing...

DAVID (*quietly*). Something – something – something – E...

Fade to black.

End of play.

Parlour Song

Jez Butterworth

☞ **WHO**   Dale, forty, and Ned, forty. (Out of context, these characters could be played younger, but bear in mind that Ned has been married for eleven years.)

☞ **WHERE**   Ned's small, suburban, new-built home, England.

☞ **WHEN**   Late summer/autumn. Present day.

☞ **WHAT HAS JUST HAPPENED**   Dale and Ned are next-door neighbours. Dale has a car-wash business and Ned works for a demolition company. Ned tells Dale that he is upset because things have been going missing from his house, most recently some cufflinks given to him by his wife, Joy. Dale is worried about Ned, who hasn't been sleeping well. One morning, having been up all night, Ned comes to see Dale and asks for help to lose weight. Dale who enjoys keeping fit has agreed to devise a programme for Ned, and, in the duologue that follows, Dale puts Ned through his paces.

☞ **WHAT TO CONSIDER**

- Ned is having a nervous breakdown. He cannot sleep for days on end. But because he is responsible for the demolition of large buildings he is not allowed to take anti-depressants or sleeping pills as they might interfere with his ability to perform his job. He must, as Dale puts it, 'white-knuckle it. Bite down. Wait for morning.'

- Ned is married to Joy. Later on in the play we discover that Joy and Dale are having an affair.

- Dale is frustrated with his work. He despises his customers in their flash cars and has a certain contempt for his employees, who are mainly from Eastern Europe.

- Dale is married to Lyn, whom we never meet. They have two children.

- The monotony of life on the estate. All the houses are identical although some of their layouts are back to front.

- The atmosphere. Beneath the veneer of this respectable suburbia lurks a longing and a menace that is at odds with its physical neatness.

- The influence of Harold Pinter. The writer has talked openly about his friendship with Pinter, and there is something 'Pinter-esque' about the way in which characters engage with one another, never fully revealing themselves.

- As with Pinter, there is also something very funny and darkly comic about the writing.

☞ **WHAT NED WANTS**

- Friendship.

- To remind himself that Joy belongs to him. (Although on the surface Ned does not know about the affair, and even admits to Dale that his sex life isn't good, make a decision about what Ned instinctively feels about his wife and the possibility that she could leave him. To what extent is this related to his desire to get fit?)

☞ **WHAT DALE WANTS**

- Friendship.

- To help.

- To be in Ned's house because he fancies Ned's wife.

☞ **WHAT THE SCENE IS ABOUT**   Male bonding carrying with it a threat of betrayal.

DALE. How you feeling?

NED. Good. Loose.

DALE. You ready?

NED. Ready to rock, Dale.

DALE. Ready to work.

NED. Bring it on, Dale. Rock and roll.

DALE. Okay. On your back.

DALE *lies on his back.* NED *does too.*

Feet six inches off the floor. Thirty seconds. Go. (*Beat.*) How's that feel?

NED. Instantly awful. Instantly wrong.

DALE. Push on.

NED. Terribly terribly wrong. Like I'm going to puke. And possibly soil myself.

DALE. Breathe. In. Out. In. Out. Twenty more seconds.

NED. My God. Make it stop. Make it stop, Dale. Please make it stop.

DALE. And rest.

NED *collapses.*

Are you okay?

NED *is panting. He starts crying.*

NED. I'm sorry, Dale. FUCK!

DALE. Ned –

NED. Fuck it.

DALE. Ned –

NED. I tensed up. I've been building up to this all day.

DALE. Calm down.

NED. I've had a shocker there.

DALE. Okay, Ned. Stand up. Ned. Relax. Stand up. We'll take it slowly.

NED. I'm sorry, Dale.

DALE. We'll start again. We'll try something else. Just do this. On the spot. (*He starts a ropeless skipping motion.*) One foot then the next. Just copy me. Until I ask you to rest. Okay?

NED. Got it.

DALE. Keep breathing. In. Out.

He starts skipping.

How is that?

NED. Fine.

DALE. Good.

NED. Just like this?

DALE. Just like that.

NED. Cor. Feels great to blow the cobwebs out.

DALE. Tell me your goals.

NED. Basically I'm looking for core fitness. Strength. Stamina. And I want to lose the tits. I'm not worried about the legs. Fuck the legs. Ignore them. I just want to look, you know. Normal. Alive. Without tits.

DALE. So just talk normally. Okay? What were you saying before? When we came in.

NED. Where were we?

DALE. Gloucester. A five-star hotel in Gloucester.

NED. Right. Gloucester. Five-star country mansion. Michelin restaurant. Spa. Four-poster. We've just had a massage, or I've had massage, and Joy's had a facial, whatever, we're feeling well blissed-out and we've got a couple of hours to kill before we go up in this balloon. (*Off* DALE*'s look.*) It's the honeymoon package. You get a four-poster bed, your food, a set number of spa treatments, and a go in a balloon. Sunset balloon trip. England at sunset. Bird's-eye view. Champagne and that.

DALE. And rest. That sounds regal. That is a regal package. Keep talking. Go again in thirty seconds.

NED. So we've got a couple of hours to kill before the balloon trip. I suggest a stroll. I suggest a walk round Gloucester. I've heard it's nice.

DALE. I've heard it's nice.

NED. The centre's nice. Olde Worlde.

DALE. That's the Romans for you.

NED. So we park and ride, and we're walking round

Gloucester, and it is nice, find the cathedral, that's nice, pop our heads in, light a candle, feeling blissed-out after the massage. Facial.

DALE. Whatever...

NED. Anyway, we're walking down the high street, and suddenly I see this thing blowing towards us down the pavement. And I bend down and pick it up and it's a fifty-pound note.

DALE. Bollocks.

NED. On my life. A nifty.

DALE. Get in!

NED. Just blowing down the street. Just blowing along the pavement.

DALE. Get in! (*Looking at watch.*) Go.

They start skipping again.

NED. So I have a shufty round and no one's looking distraught, no one's patting themselves down, having kittens, shouting for the fuzz... so I think, 'Result,' and I stick it in my pocket. So I say to Joy, you know, 'What shall we do with it?' And Joy turns to me, it's this lovely sunny day, and she turns to me, and she says this brilliant, really touching thing...

DALE. Oh no. Don't...

NED. What?

DALE stops.

DALE. She didn't. Tell me she didn't make you hand it in.

NED. Wait. Wait. No. She doesn't. She doesn't say that. She says... She says this fantastically romantic thing.

NED stops.

She says that it's a sign. From the gods. From God. Or whatever, blessing our nuptials. And she said to honour the gods, whatever, we should take half each and go and buy each other a present. Something spontaneous, you know, that we'd remember for ever, to remember this moment by. Like if you saw it in ten years' time or whatever, it would nourish us.

You know, when you think of... Just two people... in Gloucester... walking down the street...

DALE. Amazing. Magical.

NED. Just two normal people, find this money...

DALE. Get in!

NED. It's amazing. And then she says that...

DALE. It's a moment. It becomes a moment...

NED. Spontaneous –

DALE. With the money.

NED. Exactly. But it's not about the money.

DALE. Ned. Come on. Of course it's not. It's the magical...

NED. Exactly.

DALE. The magical mystery...

NED. Exactly. So we buy a Yorkie, something, Juicy Fruit, break it for change, and agree to meet back in an hour outside Argos.

DALE. I like this. I like this story.

They start skipping again.

NED. So here I am, walking around Gloucester with this big smile on my face, thinking, this is great. I am a man. On his honeymoon. I'm on my own but it's a lovely day, and I'm somewhere in this old town, and there's a woman walking around performing this magical task, on a quest to honour me. And I shall honour her.

DALE. Plus you've got the balloon ride to look forward to.

NED. Yeah, but I'm not thinking about the balloon ride at this point.

DALE. Of course not. You're lost in the moment. You're in the zone. I like this story. I like it a lot.

NED. So I start browsing. Pop in a couple of antique shops, because my first thought was get her something old. I just thought. Gloucester. Olde Worlde. Something classic. Something with soul.

DALE. With…

NED. With a past…

DALE. Character…

NED. A treasure… Exactly. I'm looking at all these bits and bobs. Trinkets, whatnot, but nothing's leaping out.

DALE. Whoops.

NED. I go from shop to shop. Nothing's leaping out.

DALE. I didn't like to say but you're going to struggle. In most antique shops with twenty-five sheets –

NED. I can't find anything…

DALE. What are we talking, realistically? Some old bottle? Some tin? 'It's filled with the patina of a bygone era.' Really. It's a piece of leather, you nit. It's a leather strap. And, you don't even know what it's off. Can I stop you, Ned? Two words. Victoria's Secrets.

NED. What?

DALE. If that was me with twenty-five sheets I'd get straight up Victoria's Secrets. Up the minty end. Get something really cheap and minty.

NED. Dale –

DALE. It's my honeymoon, Ned. There's no better time. 'There you go, love. I'll give you something to… fuckin'… nourish…' (*Beat.*) Ignore me. Please. Carry on. Please. I like this story. Ignore me.

Beat. NED *sighs. Soldiers on.*

NED. Now I don't know Gloucester. So I go round this one corner, and suddenly, the shops have stopped. I've run out of shops.

DALE. And rest.

DALE *stops.* NED *too.*

NED. I'm walking out of Gloucester. And I don't know why, but I didn't turn round. I just kept on walking. It's just petrol stations and roundabouts. Then the countryside. It's like I'm in a dream. But I can't stop walking. (*Beat.*) So I'm at this roundabout, fourth or fifth out of town. I come across this yard. And it's just this Portakabin, and this old bloke selling all these objects. Stone things. Things made out of stone. Wood things. Garden seats. Benches. And I'm suddenly drawn to this blue tarpaulin. And this is mad, but I thought, whatever it is I'm getting her, it's under that blue tarpaulin over there, in the rain. So I go over. And I lift the tarpaulin. And underneath, there's this beautiful, soapstone birdbath. Really simple, but beautiful. Not fussy, just beautifully proportioned. Simple. Perfect. So I knock on the Portakabin and I ask the man how much it is for the birdbath. And he says it's twenty-five pounds. (*Beat.*) On my life. That birdbath, the one over there, under the blue tarp, is twenty-five pound.

Pause.

DALE. Did you haggle?

Pause.

NED. What?

DALE. You didn't haggle?

NED. You're missing the point, Dale. It's twenty-five pounds.

Pause.

DALE. Of course. The fuckin'… The magical mystery twenty-five pounds.

NED. Exactly. It's perfect. So I buy it. But now I've got ten minutes to lug it all the way back into Gloucester. It weighs a fucking ton.

DALE. Fuckin'… Rocky. Go on, my son.

NED. I'm telling you, Dale. It weighs A TON.

DALE. Fuck off. It's the magic birdbath. It's light as a feather.

NED. It weighs a fucking ton.

DALE. I don't care. Put your back into it.

NED. I've got to dead lift a stone birdbath half a mile back
into town. So I get back there, absolutely shagged –

DALE. Sweating like a dogger…

NED. Pouring… pouring with sweat and I show it her. And
she looks at it, and I know straight away it's perfect. She's
got tears in her eyes. And when we moved into our house,
the first thing we did, we put that birdbath in the garden.
And on that first morning when we woke up, there was this
pair of chaffinches perched on it, drinking from it. And
every single morning when we woke up, we'd go and sit by
the window, before breakfast and watch the birds. Robins,
finches, warblers, tits, we'd get up really early in the
morning, on a spring morning, we'd watch the birds
splashing in the water, watch them preening, dancing for
each other, in little pairs, each pair perfect. And each year,
the birds came back, and each year it was the same. (*Pause.*)
Yeah. So anyway, I come out this morning, and it's gone.
It's… the birthbath has gone. There's just a white patch of
grass. It's disappeared.

Pause.

DALE. Ned –

NED. It's a birdbath, Dale. A twenty-five-quid birdbath. Our
fence is eight foot high. The gate's padlocked. It's a
soapstone birdbath. It weighs a fucking ton. I should know.
I've lugged it clean across Gloucester.

Pause. DALE's *watch alarm goes off.*

DALE. And rest. (*Pause.*) How long have you been married,
Ned?

NED. Eleven years.

DALE. How are things?

NED. Things?

DALE. Things.

Beat.

NED. Things. (*Beat.*) Good.

DALE. Good.

NED. Good.

DALE. Good. I'm just kicking the tyres.

NED. Exactly. Good. (*Nods.*)

Pause.

DALE. Recently…?

Pause.

NED. Recently? Recently. (*Nods.*) Recently less good. Recently… not so good. Recently not good.

DALE. Good.

Silence.

NED. Few years back… We used to spend all day in bed. Drinking tea. Playing Scrabble. Then… you know… Between games. All day long. Five, sometimes six games of Scrabble. Sometimes we'd play Sexy Scrabble. If you could spell it, you could have it. I once got forty-five points for 'blowjob' on a triple-word score.

DALE *laughs.* NED *laughs. He stops laughing.*

Then we stopped. We haven't played in years. I'm not sure I'd even remember the rules.

Pause.

DALE. Year or two back. Lyn and me. In the boudoir. Major tumbleweed.

NED. Whoops.

DALE. Move along. Nothing to see.

NED. Whoops-a-daisy.

DALE. In the end I bought this tape. This doctor lady. New approaches. Techniques. I used to listen to it on the way to the car wash. I've still got it somewhere. I could dig it out.

NED. Thanks, Dale. I don't think so.

DALE. If you change your mind. But I warn you. This
doctor lady. She's dirty. She's deeply filthy. Medical
website? Not a bit of it. There's stuff on there would make
a sailor blush.

NED. Thanks, Dale.

DALE. Well, if you change your mind.

Pause.

What did she get you?

NED. What?

DALE. With the magic twenty-five pound.

Beat.

NED. A tie. (*Pause.*) A tie with air balloons on.

The Pride

Alexi Kaye Campbell

☞ **WHO** Philip and Oliver, both mid-thirties, middle-class, homosexual.

☞ **WHERE** Philip's apartment, London.

☞ **WHEN** 1958.

☞ **WHAT HAS JUST HAPPENED** Philip is unhappily married to Sylvia. He is gay but in denial. When he meets her friend and colleague, Oliver, he is forced to confront his feelings of attraction. But the practice of homosexuality is illegal, and Philip cannot cope with the shame he feels. Oliver is braver. He is in love with Philip and would prefer to own up to it than live a lie. In the duologue that follows, despite agreeing to the contrary, Oliver has come to see Philip.

☞ **WHAT TO CONSIDER**

- Oliver is a writer of children's stories. He is well travelled and has spent time in Athens and the Lebanon, places associated historically with the open practice of homosexuality. Philip, on the other hand, considers himself dull by comparison. Despite dreaming about visiting Africa he jokes that he has never made it further than Brighton.

- When Philip was twenty-one his father died, followed two years later by his brother in a car accident. Philip was left to take care of his mother and sister and to run the family business, buying and selling property – a job he hates. Decide to what extent this has shaped him and goes part way to explaining his lack of courage and overall sense of being stuck.

- The duologue forms the beginning of a much longer scene between the two men. Read the play to see how it concludes.

- The play tells the story of two sets of characters, both with the same names, from 1958 and from 2008. It cleverly explores the different social pressures on gay men (and the women in their lives) between the two time frames.

☞ **WHAT PHILIP WANTS**

(Note how he is conflicted.)

On the surface:

- For Oliver to leave.
- To be rid of his homosexuality. (Make a decision about whether he really feels this way or whether it is society that dictates his feelings of self-loathing and disgust.)

Below the surface:

- To have sex with Oliver.

☞ **WHAT OLIVER WANTS**

- To express his love for Philip both emotionally and physically.
- To encourage Philip to own up to his feelings and to be true to himself.
- To be with Philip.

☞ **WHAT THE SCENE IS ABOUT**   A time when homosexuals were forced underground, desperation, repression, impossibility, ignorance; (and on the other hand) the inability to crush the human spirit, the fact that the truth will always out.

☞ **NB**   This play offers a number of other duologues from which to choose.

PHILIP. Hello.

OLIVER. I'm sorry.

PHILIP. You're drenched.

OLIVER. Yes.

   Pause.

   I wasn't planning to come. We said…

PHILIP. We said we wouldn't meet.

OLIVER. I know.

PHILIP. We said we'd try not to talk to each other.

OLIVER. Yes.

PHILIP. I think we both agreed it wasn't a good idea.

OLIVER. I know.

Pause.

PHILIP. You're drenched.

OLIVER. I was absent-minded.

PHILIP. Soaking.

OLIVER. I left my umbrella in the library.

PHILIP. Well, you'd better come in.

OLIVER *enters. He hovers.*

OLIVER. I'm sorry.

PHILIP. Sylvia's in Wimbledon staying with a friend. She'll be back tomorrow.

OLIVER. I know. We spoke on the telephone. That's why I came.

PHILIP. I don't think it's a good idea.

OLIVER. I needed to talk to you, Philip.

PHILIP. I didn't realise there was anything else to say.

OLIVER. Just one last time. And then I won't bother you.

Pause.

PHILIP. Well, you'd better have a seat.

OLIVER. Thank you.

They sit facing each other. There is a long pause before OLIVER *starts talking.*

I wanted…

PHILIP. What?

OLIVER. Nothing. I thought… I hoped…

PHILIP. You hoped what?

Pause.

OLIVER. I walked across the park. It was pouring with rain. I was forgetful. I'd been in the library. Trying to write. But I couldn't. I couldn't write. It's as if I don't know what I want to write. What I have to write. I left. To come here. But I was forgetful. I forgot my umbrella.

PHILIP. Yes.

OLIVER. I couldn't… I know we said… but I couldn't…

PHILIP. You couldn't do what?

OLIVER. All my life I've been waiting for some sort of confirmation that I'm not alone.

PHILIP. Yes.

OLIVER. When it comes, when that confirmation comes, you can't… I can't – I had to come here. And see you. I'm sorry.

PHILIP. For God's sake.

Pause.

OLIVER. It's funny. I thought I knew.

PHILIP. Knew what?

OLIVER. Knew what it meant to be lonely. To be alone. I thought I knew.

PHILIP. What do you mean?

OLIVER. But now. Now I know.

A long pause.

PHILIP. What is it you want to say to me?

OLIVER. That I love you.

PHILIP. Please don't say that again. I find it absurd.

OLIVER. I have no choice. It isn't a choice.

PHILIP. We agreed. You said… I asked you not to talk like that.

OLIVER. I love you so much.

PHILIP. Stop saying those words.

OLIVER. At night, I can't sleep. I see your face. I hear your voice.

PHILIP. Stop it.

OLIVER. When we were together, the last time, when we were together it did feel, didn't it, as if… as if. Did it not feel to you as if all of a sudden, everything, everything you *were* and are…

PHILIP. No.

OLIVER. I miss you.

PHILIP. I'd rather you left.

OLIVER. No. Please. One moment. Please let me stay for a moment.

Pause.

These four months… I understood something.

PHILIP. You understood what?

OLIVER. I used to think I was a sexual deviant. I used to –

PHILIP. Please, Oliver.

OLIVER. There was a place. Where certain men went. Where they went.

PHILIP. I don't want to hear this.

OLIVER. One of those places. I went. I stood outside. I watched. A part of me longed to go in. I can't lie to you, Philip. I longed and yearned to go in.

PHILIP. Please.

OLIVER. I used to think it was just a sexual lust. A physical need. A deviation.

PHILIP. It *is* a deviation.

OLIVER. That if I met the right girl, that if I married, if I had children, the physical need, the *sexual* need would stop. That if I loved a woman, if I could learn to love a woman, the physical need… I could learn to live without that.

PHILIP. It is a deviation.

OLIVER. That it would go away. That I could fight it.

PHILIP. That's right.

OLIVER. But then, when I met you…

PHILIP. You *can* fight it.

OLIVER. I knew it was more than that.

Pause.

That it was everything I am. Not something I can put away. Not just one part of me.

Pause.

When we were together. The times we met. All those times. When we talked.

PHILIP. We've been over this.

OLIVER. I realised that it was more. And that what I slowly learnt…

PHILIP. For God's sake…

OLIVER. Was that what happens between two people can be sacred. And important. And that it doesn't matter who those two people are.

Pause.

I remember being a boy. I remember having this dark, secret knowledge of what I pined for. Of who I was. It kept me up at nights. I was terrified. Everything, everyone, told me it was wrong.

PHILIP. It *is* wrong.

OLIVER. I thought so too. I believed that if the whole world told me so, the whole world must be right. Who was I to question that?

PHILIP. I don't see what it is you're trying to say.

OLIVER. I'm saying that when I met you, when I fell in love with you… I knew that it was true. That the world *was* wrong. That what I felt was honest and pure and good.

Pause.

I went in, Philip. Into one of those places I just told you about.

Pause.

I didn't care. I needed to go. I needed to feel… what it was like. My whole body, my whole being craved it. So I went. It was as if I was watching myself. There were men… there was this one man and he… I didn't know him. He didn't know me. We barely talked. Just a word. We didn't even really look at each other. And then… then it was as if I wasn't quite there. It was over in a couple of minutes. But it was as if I wasn't really myself. As if I was watching. Like a bystander. A witness. I can't describe it.

PHILIP. I think you should leave, Oliver.

OLIVER. But then when I… when we… it wasn't, it *isn't* the same. Because, you see, there was something *else*, Philip. We had spoken and I felt that I knew something of who you were. Your fears. Your loneliness. Your wants. I saw in your eyes, that you too, like me, are a good man.

PHILIP. A good man?

OLIVER. Yes, Philip, a good man. A *good* man. A good man. And it was the first time, when we were together, when we were embracing that I felt that I had a pride. A pride for the person I was.

PHILIP. Is this what you needed to tell me?

OLIVER. Yes, I suppose it is. I suppose I needed to tell you that what happened between us is not the same thing. Not the same as that place I went to.

PHILIP. It is the same. You're deceiving yourself. It's wrong.

OLIVER. And I thought that some of those men, if only you had seen them you would know what I mean, that some of those men, hovering, waiting in that dim flickering light, some of those men would also choose this, that maybe that's what many of them want, but because they don't know where… *how* to find it, and because they have been told that this is who they are, that they are these men who stand waiting to touch someone, to touch another man's skin, that they've believed that's *all* they are, but that what they want, what they really want is more than that, what they want is what we can have... an intimacy with someone they can hold on to for a while, that what they want more than anything is to be able to *see* them, to look at them, to look into their eyes and to *know* them. And be known.

PHILIP. Have you finished?

OLIVER. The way we know each other. Because from the minute I met you it felt as if you were the only person who had ever known my real name.

PHILIP. How do you mean?

OLIVER. As if we spoke the same language.

PHILIP. Like in your story.

OLIVER. Yes. Like in my story.

Pause.

PHILIP. But I don't feel the same way, Oliver.

OLIVER. Don't you?

PHILIP. No, Oliver, I don't. I don't. I don't.

Pause.

You see, Oliver, I love Sylvia. And Sylvia loves me. We're a couple and we love each other. What happened... I mean, what happened between us, between you and me, Oliver, between the two of us, that was simply a mistake. Call it what you will. A moment of weakness. A weakness. That's all.

OLIVER. But you said –

PHILIP. I may have said many things, Oliver, but unfortunately I probably didn't mean them. You see, I wasn't being myself. I was like a man possessed. I want you to understand though that I hold nothing against you. No rancour, no spite. I have some affection for you. I believe you are a decent man. I don't believe you influenced me or tempted me in any way or that your motives were malicious. I was as responsible as you were. We both made a mistake. That's all. I wish you well, Oliver. There are no hard feelings. But the memory of what happened… now that I seem to have regained my senses, the memory of what happened between us, of the things that happened between us, that memory fills me with shame. And disgust.

OLIVER. Disgust?

PHILIP. You came here today to persuade me that what we felt for each other, what you felt for me was noble and pure.

OLIVER. I did.

PHILIP. Well, you can feel that for me as a friend. And I can do likewise. I can like you and respect you, *try* to respect you, as a friend. But the other thing… that thing that you talk about… that place, those people.

OLIVER. What about them?

PHILIP. Those men… the ones you so eloquently described, Oliver. They are not like me and I am not like them. If you want me to be honest, Oliver, if you want to know the honest truth, I despise them. That isn't too strong a word. I have to be honest with you. I pity and despise them. I've seen them… I *see* them, I notice them in a crowd, on a bus, on the street and they disgust me. The way they walk, the way they look at you, all in the same way. I'm not like that, Oliver. And I don't think you are either. So we must put this behind us. It's for the best. I promise you it's for the best.

OLIVER. Is it?

PHILIP. One day you'll thank me. You'll understand that I did this to protect you in some way. From yourself. You'll understand that in my own, strange way it was my gift to you. My parting gift.

A long pause.

OLIVER. I suppose I should leave.

PHILIP. Yes.

Pause.

OLIVER. She knows, Philip.

PHILIP. Knows what?

OLIVER. She knows everything. About you. She knows everything about you, Philip.

PHILIP. How do you mean?

OLIVER. About what keeps you up at night. About the stirrings of your heart. The many things you're frightened of. The lonely thoughts you have. You had said to me that what made her such a wonderful actress were these two qualities she had – her empathy and her imagination. They are the same qualities that make her wise and generous. The qualities that make her know you better than you know yourself. And you have to now – because you will not be offered another opportunity – you have to now ask yourself why it is you repay her with the worst possible deception. And I'm not talking about us. About what happened between us. I'm talking about the opposite – I'm talking about your refusal to acknowledge it for what it really is.

PHILIP. Please don't talk about Sylvia to me.

OLIVER. Why not?

PHILIP. I don't want her talked about in this way. Between us, like this. I don't want us to discuss the subject of my wife.

OLIVER. Do you honestly think it's easy for me? I care about her. Deeply.

PHILIP. I don't want to talk about it.

OLIVER. But then I understood that this is what she wanted. Not *this*. Not how things are now. But us. The meeting. That is what she wanted.

PHILIP. You're insane.

OLIVER. She brought us together, Philip. I know that she brought us together.

PHILIP. You're mad.

OLIVER. Maybe not consciously, maybe not in full awareness of what she was doing. But I can put my hand on my heart and swear that Sylvia brought us together.

Pause.

I wonder when you first started thinking of emigrating.

PHILIP. Emigrating?

OLIVER. Yes. Emigrating. You mentioned it. The night I met you. Sylvia said the flat was strewn with books on Africa.

PHILIP. What has that to do with anything?

OLIVER. So I was wondering when it was that you started having that dream. Seventeen, eighteen, when? Maybe when you were becoming a man. Discovering yourself. Who you really were and what it was you wanted from your life. The open plains, you thought. The open plains of Africa. Not a bad place. I can see you there. This country is small. You need somewhere bigger. Somewhere to breathe. So you set off. I can see you. You said you never got further than Brighton, but I can see you miles, miles away. Across the cold waters of the Channel, down across the Mediterranean, down in Africa where you long to be. What are you doing there? Farming? Hunting game? Teaching? I suppose it doesn't really matter. In that sort of place, under that kind of sky you'll eventually discover what it is you're there for. In your own time.

PHILIP. Oliver.

OLIVER. I won't see you again then.

PHILIP. No.

OLIVER. That's what you want.

PHILIP. That's what we both need. To continue. To return to things as they were.

OLIVER. So what is the point?

PHILIP. The point?

OLIVER. What is the point of this stupid, painful life if not to be honest? If not to stand up for what one is in the core of one's being?

PHILIP. I don't know. I don't know.

OLIVER. Something's happened to me, Philip. I can't go back. Not to how things were before.

PHILIP. What do you mean?

OLIVER. Don't worry, I'm not expecting you to come with me. I'm not expecting anything any more. Not from you.

PHILIP. I'm sorry.

OLIVER. You're weak, Philip.

PHILIP. I wasn't…

OLIVER. What?

PHILIP. It isn't that…

OLIVER. Tell me.

PHILIP. No. Nothing.

OLIVER. Please tell me.

PHILIP. It isn't easy. It isn't easy.

Pause.

I wish I'd never met you. I wish she'd never brought you here.

OLIVER. Who are you?

PHILIP. I don't know. Not any more.

OLIVER. You've never known. This was your chance to find out. But you're not strong enough. You'll die, Philip, not knowing who you are.

PHILIP. Be quiet.

OLIVER. What a foolish, sad way to live a life.

Suddenly, PHILIP *strikes him across the face. It is a reflex; the reaction of a cornered animal.* PHILIP *is as shocked as* OLIVER, *who reels. There is some blood in the mouth.*

PHILIP. I'm sorry. Oh, God, I'm so sorry, Oliver. I'm so sorry.

He moves towards him; OLIVER flinches.

Let me see.

OLIVER *lets him.*

I'm so sorry, I'm so sorry, I'm so sorry.

OLIVER. It's all right. I'm fine.

PHILIP. I'm so sorry. I didn't… I'm so sorry…

OLIVER. I'm fine. Really, I'm fine.

And then, PHILIP *begins to cry. He collapses into* OLIVER's *arms and begins to sob like a child.*

PHILIP. I'm sorry, I'm sorry, I'm sorry.

OLIVER. It's all right, Philip, it's all right.

OLIVER *comforts him. Then, a kiss. But* OLIVER *tries to remain tender.* PHILIP *has been taken over by something else – there is something urgent, aggressive stirring in him.*

OLIVER. Wait, Philip, wait.

PHILIP. No.

A struggle of sorts as PHILIP *pulls* OLIVER *over towards the sofa – his movement becoming more violent. He begins to pull at their clothes.*

OLIVER. No, Philip. Not like this. Not now. Not here. Wait.

PHILIP. Why not now? Why not here? It's what you want, isn't it? It's what you want me to be, isn't it?

PHILIP *has become violent. He throws* OLIVER *down.* OLIVER *is resisting.* PHILIP *unzips his own trousers and has managed to pull* OLIVER's *halfway down. He mounts him with* OLIVER *resisting at first, then succumbing. In just a few, frenzied seconds he has ejaculated and the noise he makes at the moment of orgasm is a terrible, anguished cry of release. They lie on the floor for some time –* PHILIP *hiding his face in shame,* OLIVER *hiding his.*

Eventually, PHILIP *stands. Quietly, methodically, he dresses and leaves the room.* OLIVER *does not move. He is lying on the floor, his face down against it.* PHILIP *returns a minute or so later. He pours himself a drink and sits. He lights a cigarette. A moment passes.*

Slowly, painfully, OLIVER *gets up and begins to rearrange his clothing. A minute or two pass in complete silence.*

I knew you should never have come here.

Pause.

I think you should leave, Oliver. This thing… this thing is…

I want you to leave and never come back.

OLIVER *moves slowly across the room to the door. He does not look at* PHILIP. *He looks down at the floor. He opens the door, then pauses.*

OLIVER. I'm sorry… I…

He pauses, confused. As if trying to gather his thoughts.

What I… the thing… I… was…

Pause.

I'm sorry. I thought I knew you.

He leaves the room, closing the door behind him.

PHILIP *does not move. He remains seated, drinking his whisky and smoking his cigarette.*

Regeneration

From the book by Pat Barker
Adapted by Nicholas Wright

☞ **WHO**   Siegfried Sassoon, soldier and poet, thirty, and Wilfred Owen, soldier and poet, twenty-four

☞ **WHERE**   Siegfried's room, Craiglockhart Army Hospital, Scotland.

☞ **WHEN**   1917, during the First World War.

☞ **WHAT HAS JUST HAPPENED**   In 1917 Siegfried Sassoon was admitted to Craiglockhart army hospital in order to avoid a court martial. He had written a Declaration in which he was highly critical of the war and its continuation. His friend, the poet Robert Graves, managed to pull some strings at the War Office, and it was agreed that Sassoon, who had returned home, should be treated as a mental-health patient, along with other shell-shocked officers, rather than be publicly disciplined. Despite being fit for battle, he was sent to the hospital in Scotland where he received pioneering treatment from Captain Rivers, who was a specialist in nerve regeneration. Also in the hospital was poet Wilfred Owen, who we know from history was greatly influenced by Sassoon before his return to the war and his untimely death in 1918. In the duologue that follows, Owen, already an admirer of Sassoon's, introduces himself.

☞ **WHAT TO CONSIDER**

- The play is a stage adaptation of Pat Barker's novel, *Regeneration*. It is based on true events at Craiglockhart army hospital, where returning officers were treated for nervous disorders relating to their experiences in the trenches.

- Take time to research the lives of Sassoon and Owen and the appalling conditions that the soldiers suffered during the First World War.

- Although a fine and brave soldier, Sassoon became angry at the way in which the war was waged and at its pointless loss of life.

- Sassoon was gay, and there is the strong suggestion in the play that Owen is in love with him.

- Sassoon is confident. He is described in the play as: 'poised', 'fit', 'handsome' and 'assured'.

- Owen is less so. He is described in the play as: 'not tall, with a warm voice and a slight stammer'.

☞ WHAT WILFRED WANTS

- To meet his hero.

- Some recognition from Sassoon of his own writing.

- Intimacy with Sassoon, emotionally and intellectually. (To what extent is the request for a contribution to *The Hydra* a convenient excuse for Owen's approach?)

☞ WHAT SIEGFRIED WANTS

- Friendship and a sharing with someone he considers to be of equal intellect.

☞ WHAT THE SCENE IS ABOUT   Surviving war, friendship in adversity, the attraction of a young man for a man slightly older, the power of poetry to express the unspeakable, the meeting of two great minds not unlike that of Byron and Shelley.

☞ NB   This play offers a number of other duologues from which to choose.

Evening. SIEGFRIED, *in a purple dressing gown, is cleaning a golf club. There's a knock at the door.*

SIEGFRIED. Hello?

The door opens cautiously. WILFRED *is there.*

WILFRED. Lieutenant Sassoon?

SIEGFRIED. Yes?

WILFRED. I'm, I'm sorry to disturb you.

SIEGFRIED. That's all right. Come in.

WILFRED *does.*

WILFRED. I wondered, would you... would you sign your book for me, please?

(*It's a slim book of verse.*) *The Old Huntsman.*

SIEGFRIED. Yes, of course.

He takes it.

WILFRED. I've brought a pen.

He hands it to SIEGFRIED.

SIEGFRIED. What name shall I write?

WILFRED. Susan Owen. My mother.

SIEGFRIED *looks at a page.*

SIEGFRIED. Page forty-two. Are you quite sure that she wants to read that 'Bert's gone syphilitic'? I had trouble even getting the publishers to print that.

WILFRED. I don't think it will come as any surprise to her. I tell her everything in my letters. Don't you?

SIEGFRIED. I think I've shocked her quite enough without any more searing revelations.

WILFRED. She must be very upset about your being in hospital.

SIEGFRIED. Not at all. I think it's one of her few comforts.

WILFRED. Really?

SIEGFRIED. Yes, she'd far rather have a son who was here in Dottyville, than a son who was being called a pacifist. You know why I'm here, I suppose?

WILFRED. Yes, I read your Declaration.

SIEGFRIED. What did you think of it?

WILFRED. I agreed with every word.

SIEGFRIED. I'm glad that somebody did.

He hands the book back to WILFRED.

WILFRED. Thank you. Um...

He gets more books out of his bag.

...there should be five altogether.

SIEGFRIED. Five? Has the War Office put it on a recommended reading list?

WILFRED. That's not very likely, is it? No, they're for my family.

He hands SIEGFRIED *a book.*

SIEGFRIED. Who's this one for?

WILFRED. My brother Harold. He's a midshipman in the Royal Navy Reserve.

SIEGFRIED (*writing*). Harold Owen?

WILFRED. Yes.

SIEGFRIED *signs and they exchange books.*

SIEGFRIED. And this one?

WILFRED. Mary Owen. My sister. She's just turned twenty-two. And…

SIEGFRIED *signs and they exchange books.*

…this one's for my cousin. Leslie Gunston.

He looks over SIEGFRIED's *shoulder to check his spelling.*

G–U… that's right.

SIEGFRIED. Where is he stationed?

WILFRED. He isn't stationed anywhere. He has a mitral murmur in his heart. Well, that's the story. I'm not very admiring of it. But we're still friends. We show each other our poems, in fact.

He glances at SIEGFRIED, *hoping for some acknowledgement of his poetry-writing, but it's not forthcoming.* SIEGFRIED *indicates the book that* WILFRED *is holding:*

SIEGFRIED. And the last one is for you?

WILFRED. Yes.

SIEGFRIED. Hand it over.

WILFRED *does, and then stays looking over* SIEGFRIED's *shoulder.*

Sit down.

WILFRED *sits.*

I can't sign it until you tell me your name.

WILFRED. Oh, I'm sorry. It's Owen. Wilfred Owen.

SIEGFRIED *signs.*

I've been wanting to meet you ever since I heard you were here. But I didn't have the nerve to just, just wander up to you and, you know, parley in a casual way. That's where your book came in. But it's true that I'm a great admirer of it. I like 'The Death-bed' best.

SIEGFRIED. I was quite pleased with it.

WILFRED. I like 'The Redeemer' too.

SIEGFRIED *flips through the book, in the way that writers do.* WILFRED *recites:*

'He faced me, reeling in his weariness,
Shouldering his load of planks, so hard to bear.
I say that He was Christ, who wrought to bless…'

I've been wanting to write something like that for years.

SIEGFRIED. Don't you think the Christ reference is rather lazy-minded? Jesus didn't go around sticking bayonets into Germans' stomachs.

He hands the book back to WILFRED.

Was that tactless of me? You're not a Christian, are you?

WILFRED. I was when I was younger, but I'm not any more. I don't know what I am. I know I wouldn't want a religion that couldn't face up to the facts.

SIEGFRIED. What facts?

WILFRED. Well, if you call yourself a Christian, you can't leave out the bits that bother you, can you? If I *were* a Christian, I'd have to be a pacifist as well.

SIEGFRIED. And you're *not* a pacifist?

WILFRED. No, I'm not. Are you?

SIEGFRIED. No, I'm a soldier.

WILFRED. It's funny. All the time in France, I never thought about things like that.

SIEGFRIED. No, one's usually too busy to bother with ethical questions.

WILFRED. Or psychological ones.

SIEGFRIED. Or mystical ones.

WILFRED. That isn't always the case, though, is it?

SIEGFRIED. No?

WILFRED. No, I don't think so. Sometimes when you're alone, in the trenches, at night, you get the sense of something quite ancient there. As though there had always been trenches there. One trench we held, it had skulls packed into the earth all up the side. Like mushrooms. And it was easier to believe they were men from the Duke of Marlborough's army in seventeen-something, than to accept that they'd all been alive in the last two years. It's as if all other wars had somehow... distilled themselves into this war, and that made it into something you... almost couldn't challenge. Like a deep and powerful voice saying, 'Run along, little man. Be thankful if you survive.'

Embarrassed, he feels that it's time to go. He takes up the books.

Thank you for these. Oh, that reminds me. I'm editor of the hospital magazine. It's called *The Hydra*. I was wondering if you could let us have a poem to include in it?

SIEGFRIED. I probably can. I'll look for something.

WILFRED. Thank you. We'll appreciate it no end.

He's about to go, but the conversation feels somehow unfinished.

SIEGFRIED. I was going up with the rations one night and I saw the artillery pieces against the skyline and the flares going up. Just like one sees them every night. Only it seemed to me that I was seeing it from the future. I realised that a hundred years from now, they'll still be ploughing up skulls, and I felt that I was in the future, looking back to the way we were that night. I think I saw our ghosts.

Pause.

Did you say that *you're* a writer?

WILFRED. I didn't exactly, but I do write.

SIEGFRIED. Poetry?

WILFRED. Yes. Nothing in print yet.

SIEGFRIED. You could always show me some of your stuff, if you really want to.

WILFRED *laughs, amused by* SIEGFRIED*'s manifest lack of enthusiasm.*

WILFRED. You don't have to torture yourself!

SIEGFRIED. No, I mean it!

WILFRED. They *are* quite short.

SIEGFRIED. Yes, the war doesn't lend itself to epics.

WILFRED. Oh, I don't write about the war.

SIEGFRIED. Why not?

WILFRED. I… I've always thought the poetry *I* can write, is… it's a presumptuous thing to say, but I like to aim at something beautiful. I think the war's too ugly to write about.

SIEGFRIED. Isn't that like having a religion that can't face up to the facts?

WILFRED *thinks, puzzled.*

WILFRED. Maybe.

SIEGFRIED. You could bring me a poem next time we meet.

WILFRED. Well, as a matter of fact, I've got one here.

SIEGFRIED. Let's see it.

WILFRED *produces a notebook. Opens it, passes it over.*

WILFRED. I know I said they were all short, but this one's quite long. I wrote it for Captain Brock as part of my therapy.

SIEGFRIED *looks at the title.*

SIEGFRIED (*reads*). 'Antaeus'.

WILFRED. Yes.

SIEGFRIED. Why that?

WILFRED. That's what therapeutic about it. Antaeus was a giant who challenged Hercules to a wrestling match. And Hercules couldn't beat him, until he remembered that Antaeus was the son of Gaia, the goddess of the earth. And every time that Antaeus *touched* the earth, even if only with a toe, his mother would give him his strength back. So Hercules lifted him up into the air in a great bear-hug, and that's how he beat him. Dr Brock says his patients are like Antaeus, because we've been... 'upgrounded', he calls it... by the war.

SIEGFRIED *puts the poem to one side. Looks at* WILFRED, *as though seeing him for the first time.*

SIEGFRIED. Do you ever feel like strangling Brock?

WILFRED. No, we get on very well.

SIEGFRIED. My doctor is Captain Rivers.

WILFRED. Yes, I know.

SIEGFRIED. He's going on three weeks' holiday in the morning.

WILFRED. Maybe he needs a rest.

SIEGFRIED. It makes me bloody angry. I feel betrayed. I'll just have to concentrate on how glad I'll be that he's gone. He keeps reminding me that, after the war, people are going to ask me what I did. And that I'll have to reply, 'I spent three very comfortable years in a loony bin playing golf, while most of my friends got blown to smithereens.' He knows that I'll feel a total shit.

WILFRED *takes his time thinking through the following:*

WILFRED. I think... it takes time to get back to the way you were. When you were fit and well. And *once* that happens, I think you'll probably know that it's time. It'll come to you out of a blue sky.

SIEGFRIED. What happened to you? Why are you here?

WILFRED. I was blown sideways by a shell. There was no way of getting back to the line, so I hid in a railway cutting with a piece of corrugated iron over me. The officer I was with had caught it.

SIEGFRIED. Caught it how?

WILFRED *snaps.*

WILFRED. Do you really not know what that means? He was killed. Smashed to bits! I lay there smelling his stink for three days!

SIEGFRIED. I'm sorry.

WILFRED *passes it off.*

WILFRED. It was nothing. Only I started forgetting things all over the place. No use to anyone.

Pause.

I'm sorry I yelled. What'll you, what'll you do when this is all over?

SIEGFRIED. I've got no plans. What about you?

WILFRED. I'm going to keep pigs.

SIEGFRIED. Pigs?

WILFRED. Yes. People think pigs are dirty, but that's only if they're badly kept, and they're very intelligent. We had a piglet used to knock on the kitchen door to watch my brother and me having our tea.

SIEGFRIED. Are you a country man?

WILFRED. Through and through. From Shropshire. I'm mad about animals. I used to ride all day when I was a lad.

SIEGFRIED. There are horses here. We can ride together, if you like. [...]

WILFRED. That poem for *The Hydra*. Don't forget.

SIEGFRIED. I won't. Goodnight.

WILFRED. Goodnight.

Scuttlers

Rona Munro

☞ **WHO**   Joe, a young soldier, and George, a young slum dweller, both from Manchester.

☞ **WHERE**   Prussia Street, the Ancoats district of Manchester.

☞ **WHEN**   The summer of 1882, night-time.

☞ **WHAT HAS JUST HAPPENED**   Joe, who left home to join the army, has been temporarily posted back to Manchester. Before he is moved on, Joe is desperate to get back together with his former girlfriend Susan, who in Joe's absence gave birth to their baby son. Susan is unmoved by Joe's promises of marriage and remains angry about the way Joe dumped her in the first place. In the meantime, Joe has been staying with Susan's brother George, a gang member of the Prussia Street mob. In the duologue that follows, Joe has persuaded George to let him see his son while George is preparing himself for a fight with their rival gang, the 'Tigers' of Bengal Street.

☞ **WHAT TO CONSIDER**

- 'Scuttlers' was the name given to the gang members of the Ancoats district of Manchester, who ruled the streets there in the nineteenth century.

- The Burnley spinners are all out on strike, leaving the looms empty and the mill workers, like George, temporarily without work.

- It is a hot summer; the factories are closed but the pubs have been open. Fuelled by drink and restless from unemployment, the young people are ready for a fight.

- The 'tags' that George points out are big chalk marks that have been drawn on the ground. They are the signal that the Tigers have called for a fight.

- The presence of the baby. Think how you will represent him and what he brings to the scene.

- The scene's contrasting elements. Namely, the softness and vulnerability of the baby; George's need, but also terror at having to assert himself; Joe's desire to be the man and to take responsibility; and the threat of the impending fight. What do these things smell and taste like?

- The girl running at the front of the Tigers is Joe's sister Theresa. But it is years since he last saw her, and he cannot be sure it is she. Read the play to learn more about their relationship.

- Read Rona Munro's fascinating introduction to the playscript, in which she draws a parallel between the wars of the Scuttlers and the UK riots of 2011.

☞ WHAT JOE WANTS

- To take ownership of (and to physically hold) his baby son.

- To protect George.

- To prove that he can be a good father and to show that he has become a man.

☞ WHAT GEORGE WANTS

(Note how he is conflicted.)

- To hide.

- To remain a boy.

- To conquer his fear.

- To prove his manhood.

☞ WHAT THE SCENE IS ABOUT   The nervous anticipation before a battle, growing up, masculinity, poverty and the paucity of expectation.

GEORGE *walks slowly up to the bridge, looking into the dark, down towards Jersey Street. He has the baby in his arms.*

JOE *comes up the dark street behind him.*

JOE. Thanks for this, George. Thanks, she barely let me see his face.

GEORGE *is holding the baby so he can see it.*

GEORGE. No doubt he's yours, ugly little monster.

JOE. Look at him! Look at him! He's wide awake!

GEORGE. Aye. Too hot to sleep. He never settles when it's hot like this.

JOE. He wanted to stay up to see his dad.

(*To baby.*) Didn't you? That's what it was, wasn't it?

GEORGE. Feel how thick the air is. There'll be a storm coming.

They're running all through Prussia Street territory. Must be coming up the canal.

JOE. That was how we used to do it.

(*He's still looking at the baby.*) Where is she?

GEORGE. At her work. She'll be at the dispensary all night. She doesn't mind me holding him, I'm his uncle.

JOE. What's his name?

GEORGE (*grins*). George.

JOE. Oh, you little fucker!

GEORGE. We're both named after my Uncle George really. Here.

He puts the baby in JOE*'s arms.*

JOE (*anxious*). Is he alright?

GEORGE. Course he's alright. He'll soon let you know if he's not, believe me, there'll be no doubt when he starts roaring.

JOE. He's heavy, heavy as a cannonball.

GEORGE. He's fat as one.

JOE. I'm asking you, George, have you ever seen a babe with legs like that? My boy's going to kick the world over when he's grown.

GEORGE. He's got a powerful kick, I'll give you that.

So. You've seen this?

He points out the tags.

JOE. Aye.

GEORGE. Looks like we'll have to kill all the Tigers tomorrow, Joe. Hope that won't upset you.

JOE. I told you. I'm here now.

GEORGE. Well… that's good, because I'll be leading the Prussia Street gang over the bridge tomorrow. The Tigers have called for a fight.

Beat.

JOE. How old are you now, George?

GEORGE. Sixteen.

JOE. How did you end up at the front of the Prussia Street mob?

GEORGE (*shrugs*). I won the fight.

JOE. Did you?

GEORGE. Yeah. With Harry Bold? Know him?

JOE. No.

GEORGE. Well, he were a knob, but he ran the Prussia Street gang. And he liked to push the little boys over, you know, be the big man. So I pushed back. And he were blind drunk. So I beat him. Easy.

Then I just had to front it out every time it needed fronting out. That was easy too.

JOE. Till now.

You worried you can't beat the Tigers?

GEORGE. We can wipe them out. There's hundreds of us, Joe. You haven't seen the Prussia Street boys for a while, have you? We've got two men for every Tiger. We can run them over.

JOE. So... what is it?

GEORGE *hesitates.*

GEORGE. I don't know how to do it. I don't know how to lead them out. I've never had to do that, see... How did you do it when you were a Tiger?

JOE. Just gave a good shout and started running. Don't look round to see if they're following, just keep running.

GEORGE. Right... alright... aye... easy...

JOE. You don't have to lead them out, George.

GEORGE. If I don't they'll say I'm a coward. They'll spit at me all down Prussia Street.

JOE. Are you sure you've got the numbers? Are you sure?

GEORGE. Aye. Two men for every Tiger, I promise you.

JOE. But they don't know that?

GEORGE. No, last time we fought the Tigers we were pitiful. We've three times those numbers now.

JOE. Then all you have to do is let them see that. Stand on this bridge and stamp. Let them see the army you've got. Let them hear it.

They can count heads.

There'll be some boy at the front of the Tigers even more scared than you are.

GEORGE. I'm not scared!

JOE. No shame in it, George. A fight's a frightening thing. So don't make one if you don't need to. Just don't make the move.

Let them run at you if they dare.

GEORGE. But they won't?

JOE. Well... if they do... two to one... you should beat them.

GEORGE. I'd have to be at the front, though. I've just never fought at the front, Joe. Not a whole mob.

JOE. You do what I've said, I'll be amazed if you need to. You won't need to fight this time, George. Just let them see you. That's all you'll have to do.

The baby starts to cry.

Aw fuck... what do I...?

GEORGE. Just jiggle him.

JOE tries, clumsily. It's not working. GEORGE takes over.

Give him here.

He takes the baby, quietens it expertly.

Will you walk down with us, Joe?

JOE. I promised Susan I'd keep you out of trouble, not take you out street-fighting.

GEORGE. Will you though?

JOE. I'll stand at the back, I'll be back there if you need me.

GEORGE. Thanks.

JOE. But you do what I say and you won't need me.

GEORGE. Thanks, Joe.

JOE. George, who was that girl? Running at us today?

GEORGE. What girl?

JOE. Running at the front of the Tigers?

GEORGE (*shrugs*). I don't know. Just some girl. Why? Did you know her?

JOE. I knew someone looked like her, but she wouldn't run with the Tigers, she were only a little thing, soft as a cotton ball.

GEORGE. Want me to find out?

JOE. No, no, leave it.

Sixty Five Miles
Matt Hartley

☞ **WHO**   Pete Giles, early thirties, and his brother Rich Giles, early twenties, both from Sheffield.

☞ **WHERE**   Rich's living room in the old family home in Sheffield.

☞ **WHEN**   November 2005. 11a.m.

☞ **WHAT HAS JUST HAPPENED**   This is the very first scene of the play. Pete has been released from prison, and the duologue that follows is the first time that the brothers have seen each other in nine years.

☞ **WHAT TO CONSIDER**

- Both brothers are dealing with a loss and regret of some kind. Pete is searching for the daughter he has never met and Rich is coping with his decision to split from his girlfriend, who was pregnant with his child at the time and was forced to terminate the pregnancy.

- The play is set in Sheffield and Hull. The sixty-five miles of the title is the distance between the two cities.

- Sheffield has changed in the nine years that Pete has been in prison. The once run-down town has been part of a major regeneration scheme. Pete can barely recognise it, only adding to his feelings of displacement.

☞ **WHAT PETE WANTS**

- Help, in order to find his daughter.

- To right his past wrongs.

- To assert his dominance over his younger brother, despite the shame of having been in prison.

- To be part of a family.

- Acceptance.

- Forgiveness.

☞ WHAT RICH WANTS

- To express his rage and hurt at what Pete has done, while at the same time…

- To welcome Pete back. (Despite being angry at his brother, notice how he has taken the day off to greet him and has made a cake in his honour.)

- To make the family whole. (The baking of the cake is somehow symbolic of this.)

- To find a way of forgiving his brother.

☞ WHAT THE SCENE IS ABOUT   Readjustment, brotherly rivalry, brotherly love, loss, regret, bitterness, hope, forgiveness.

☞ NB   This play offers a number of other duologues from which to choose.

PETE *stands facing* RICH, *a very small suitcase by his feet.*
Silence.

PETE. 'An't changed, 'as it?

RICH. No.

PETE. Still the same tatty wallpaper.

RICH. Yeah.

PETE. This fucking carpet.

PETE *stares round the room.*

RICH. A put a shelf up.

PETE. Yeah?

RICH. But it fell down. Was there.

PETE. Right.

RICH. 'Ardly anything on it. Just a couple of books.

PETE. Is that right?

RICH. No real pressure on the shelf. Just gave way. Think I must just be crap at DIY. So haven't bothered t'put it back up again.

PETE. Probably right. Don't want loads of fucking… /
  marks.

RICH. / Holes.

PETE. On the walls. Exactly, yeah.

RICH. Yeah.

  Silence.

PETE. Dirty though. Could do with a fucking clean, yer
  know. All this dust.

RICH. A do clean.

PETE. Make yerself ill if you don't.

  Pause.

  Feels strange. /

RICH. So it should.

PETE. / Back in this house.

  Pause.

  This fucking carpet.

RICH. Small bag.

PETE. What?

RICH. Just sayin', that's a small bag.

PETE. Are yer tekin the piss?

RICH. No, just… It's a small bag that's all.

PETE. Are you trying to make this more awkward than it
  already is?

RICH. No.

PETE. Because I don't need that.

  Pause.

RICH. Just I never seen one that small before.

PETE. What?

RICH. That. I just never seen somert so tiny. Not for clothes.

PETE. Don't'ave much stuff that's why.

RICH. Right. Right. Not much stuff, right.

PETE. That's why I've got it. This little thing. Fuckin'.
Camp little, what would you call it, suitcase? /

RICH. Handbag.

PETE. / Couple shirts. Pair of trousers. Photo or two.
Letters. That's all. Yer know? Look. Look at this. It has
this. Has a handle. Pull it up. Helps yer t'drag it. Saves yer
from carryin' it. Imagine doing that…

RICH. D'yer want me t'take it f'yer?

PETE waves the question away.

PETE. Feel like a should tek me shoes off.

RICH. Can do.

PETE. But I'm not going to. No point is the'. This fuckin'
carpet. Like tar. Like walkin' on tar. Should just rip it up.

RICH. Is that right.

PETE. My opinion anyway. Never liked it. Look at that mark.
Dirty big stain –

RICH. It's just a mark, right. Not the end of the world.

PETE. No. No, I suppose not.

Very long silence.

So.

RICH. So?

Beat.

What?

PETE. Yer know?

RICH. What?

PETE. Yer read me letter.

RICH. Only one yer sent me.

PETE. Don't be precious.

RICH. Just sayin'.

PETE. Yer read it.

RICH. Yes.

PETE. And?

RICH. Pete. Don't think it were fair.

PETE. Rich.

RICH. What you asked of me. Don't you think?

PETE. Rich.

RICH. I don't think it were fair.

PETE. Rich, don't make me spell it out.

RICH. No.

PETE. No?

RICH. No. Didn't leave an address. Nothing.

PETE. Okay, okay, okay.

   Pause.

   Okay.

RICH. Wish you 'adn't asked me t'do it.

PETE. Yer tried Emma's family?

RICH. Felt awkward. Well fuckin' awkward.

PETE. Yer tried Emma's mum?

RICH. Why you suddenly interested? Never bothered before.

PETE. Yer try Emma's mum?

RICH. No.

PETE. She still live up –

RICH. I don't even know who she is, Pete.

PETE. No, no, no.

   Beat.

   No?

RICH. No.

PETE. No, I guess yer wouldn't.

   Pause.

RICH. D'yer want some cake?

PETE. Cake?

RICH. Yeah.

PETE. Is that what the smell is?

RICH. Just tried out a recipe.

PETE. Nah, I'll be alright.

> *Silence.*

> PETE *lifts the handle on the suitcase up then pushes it back down.*

> *Silence.*

> Can I have a cup of tea though? I'd like a cup of tea.

RICH. Yer staying then?

PETE. Yeah.

RICH. Not just going to piss off.

PETE. No. Need t–

RICH. Cos your old room, that's mine now.

PETE. Right.

RICH. Has been for ages. You'll have to sleep in my old room. Bunk beds. You'll be alright with that won't you? Used t'them.

> *Silence.*

> Suppose I could get you some fresh sheets. Put them in Mum's. You'll have t'clear the stuff off it though.

PETE. Nine years.

RICH. Nine 'n'alf.

PETE. Thought yer might have grown a little.

RICH. Fuck off.

PETE. Least a couple of inches.

RICH. Grown a lot. Learned a lot.

PETE. Bit of a short-arse really.

RICH. Sorry?

PETE. Yer quite short, aren't yer?

RICH. Not short. Average mebee but not short.

PETE. 'Ow tall are yer then?

RICH. I dunno.

PETE. 'Bout five nine.

RICH. I dunno.

PETE. Mebee five eight.

RICH. I don't fuckin' know, yeah!

>*Pause.*

>Pete, yer should know. This is my house right. Yer just a guest.

>*Silence.* PETE *takes a photo off the top of the television. Stares at it. Looks at* RICH. *Looks at the photo.*

PETE. Certainly take after me mum. Same haircut. /

RICH. Fuck off.

PETE. / S'uncanny.

RICH. Fuck off.

PETE. Apart from the language on yer.

RICH. Put that back.

>RICH *puts his hand down the front of his trousers.*

>Put it back, Pete.

>PETE *does.*

PETE. Yer still stick yer hand down yer trousers when yer nervous.

RICH. I'm not nervous.

PETE. I'd rather yer were nervous than aroused.

RICH. You've got some fucking nerve.

>PETE *stares at* RICH. RICH *wavers.*

>Meant t'be at work yer know.

PETE. No.

Beat.

RICH. Well, I am. But I took the day off. Not getting holiday pay or nothing. Just took it off. Hope yer happy that I'm going t'be poorer.

PETE. I'm going t'need t'borrow yer car over the next month or so.

Pause.

RICH. Mum dunt know yer stayin' 'ere yer know?

PETE. No?

RICH. Talkin' about you still upsets her.

PETE. –

RICH. She's proud of me.

PETE. Yeah.

RICH. Thought yer should know that.

Pause.

PETE. Do you want a badge, is that what yer want?

RICH. Shut up.

PETE. Little fucking badge. Pin it t'yer shirt.

RICH. No.

PETE. Mummy's boy, written on it.

RICH. No.

PETE. Then what you fucking saying that for?

RICH *goes to puts his hands down his trousers, stops himself.*

RICH. Not funny, yer know. Not laughin'.

Pause.

Nine years and I didn't even get a fuckin' hello.

PETE. Nine years, six months, eleven days.

Pause. RICH *exits.* PETE *rubs his eyes. Stares round the room.* RICH *returns.*

What?

RICH. How do yer 'ave yer tea?

PETE. Me?

RICH. A don't have to ask meself do I. Kinda know that myself. Course you.

PETE. Yer don't remember.

RICH. Just asked yer didn't I? Surely that answers yer question.

PETE. You used to always make me my tea. On a Saturday. *Football Focus*. I'd come round. Hungover. Yer'd bring me a cup of tea.

RICH. Right.

PETE. Yer used t'do that.

RICH. I believe yer. 'N' how did yer use t'ave yer tea?

PETE. Just milk.

RICH. Right.

   RICH *goes to exit.*

PETE. But –

RICH. What?

PETE. Well, that was then.

RICH. Then?

PETE. Now a have it different.

RICH. Christ –

PETE. Just that sugar's one of the only luxuries yer can get hold of easily.

   Pause.

   Two sugars.

   RICH *exits into the kitchen.* PETE *remains standing. Looks round. Retches. Bends his knees, puts his hand over his mouth.* RICH *enters, watches* PETE *in this position. Eventually…*

   Fucking… strange, yeah…

RICH. Right.

   Long pause.

PETE. I got the train down.

RICH. Okay.

PETE. And when I got off at the station. Thought I'd got off at wrong place.

RICH. Town's changed.

PETE. Too right. Everything's shiny.

RICH. Just be grey in a few years.

PETE. And I just stood there. Staring. Not knowing what to do. Then I thought, I'm going to just smash this place up, tear it apart –

RICH. You didn't?

PETE *shakes his head.*

PETE. Just walked here instead.

RICH. Shouldn't say things like that. Especially after what you did. People believe that you'd actually do it.

PETE. –

RICH. Sit down, will yer.

PETE. What did yer say?

RICH. Why don't you sit down?

RICH *hands him a cup of tea. He has a piece of cake on a plate as well.* PETE *drinks.*

PETE. Nice.

RICH. 'Ardly rocket science, is it.

PETE. 'Arder than it looks.

RICH. It's not really, is it?

PETE. No.

RICH. Then why d'yer say it?

Pause.

PETE. Is that the cake?

RICH. One yer didn't want any of.

RICH *starts to eat the cake.*

PETE. They lettin' yer make the desserts now?

RICH. –

PETE. I'll be yer guinea pig.

RICH. –

PETE. Best try it on me. Before yer poison yer customers.

RICH. Yer do read my letters then.

PETE. Never read anythin' about yer poisonin' yer customers.

RICH. Fuck off.

PETE. I know yer a chef if that's what yer getting at.

RICH. Coulda replied t'one of them.

Silence.

Yer know yer shoulda fuckin' done. Twice. After all this time, s'not enough. Yer might as well be a stranger.

Silence. PETE *stands up and moves around the room. Stops. Cups his hands and rubs his face. Lets his hands fall to his side.*

PETE. I wanted it t'be rainin' when I got out. Wanted t'feel it. Love rain. On my skin. Freshness of it.

RICH. Not talkin' about the weather are yer? Only boring tossers speak about the weather.

PETE. I'm talking about me. Couldn't put the feelings in words. Couldn't write them down.

RICH. Coulda phoned.

PETE. Couldn't say them either.

RICH. Well, yer a bit screwed then.

PETE. I'm trying now.

Silence.

She were fifteen last week.

RICH. She probably won't even want t'see you.

PETE. Because of me there is a fifteen-year-old girl in this world. Amazes me.

RICH. Yer weren't even there when she were born.

Silence.

PETE. Life's about mistakes. Making them. Then learning.

RICH. No. That's not good enough.

PETE. We've all done things we regret. Don't go thinking you're a fucking angel.

RICH. Compared to you I'm Jesus.

PETE. I've just done things on a bigger scale.

RICH. Colossal, that's what scale.

PETE. Shut up.

RICH. You shut up.

PETE. No, you shut –

RICH. I told people that you were dead.

Beat.

PETE. What?

RICH. Wasn't going t'tell you. But I told people that you were dead. That's what I told them when they asked about my family.

PETE *starts to laugh.*

'S not funny. Truth. I did.

PETE *slowly stops to laugh.*

PETE. See you've done somert that you regret.

RICH. That doesn't keep me up at night.

PETE. No?

RICH. No.

Pause.

PETE. But somert does. Dunt it?

Pause. RICH *puts his hands down his trousers. Removes it almost instantly.*

RICH. A think yer should go 'n'and 'ave a lie-down.

PETE. 'Ave a shower.

RICH. Freshen up.

Long pause.

PETE. You stayin' in?

RICH. Not fuckin' workin', am I?

PETE *starts to exit, carrying his suitcase. Stops. Turns back round.*

PETE. Rich.

RICH. Yeah?

Silence.

That bag is the biggest fuckin' joke. Look a right prick.

Pause. PETE *exits.* RICH *stands. Fade.*

The Three Lions

William Gaminara

☞ **WHO**   David Cameron, British Prime Minister, forty-four, and David Beckham, celebrity football player, thirty-five. (Because the scene is something of a comedy sketch, the duologue can be played by much younger actors.)

☞ **WHERE**   A smart, medium-sized, en suite room in a Zurich hotel, Switzerland.

☞ **WHEN**   1st December 2010.

☞ **WHAT HAS JUST HAPPENED**   It is the night before the announcement of the host nation for the 2018 FIFA World Cup. David Cameron has arrived at the hotel in Zurich where he will be meeting David Beckham and Prince William to discuss their strategy for tomorrow morning's bid. He has been given the wrong room (he asked for a double and has been put in a twin room with two single beds) and while he waits for the hotel to sort out a new room for him, David Beckham walks in. The following duologue is their first meeting.

☞ **WHAT TO CONSIDER**

- The fine line between playing the 'persona' and the 'real person'. In many ways these characters need to be accurately impersonated, but they must also strike us as real people and not just as caricatures.

- What happens when two famous people meet or spend time together? It is obvious that when most people initially meet they know very little about one another. How might it be if you are world-famous thinking you already know a lot about the other world-famous person?

- Might you be more relaxed because you share fame or, as in David Cameron's case, might you feel a little intimidated at the thought of spending time with a sporting hero?

- How does Beckham appear with Cameron? In this portrayal, is he even interested in politics?

- There are some brilliant scenes between Cameron, Beckham and Prince William. You might like to team up with a third actor for these.

☞ **WHAT CAMERON WANTS**

- To start work on their bid. (Notice how hard it is for him to get Beckham to concentrate.)

☞ **WHAT BECKHAM WANTS**

- To look good for tomorrow.

☞ **WHAT THE SCENE IS ABOUT**   Class difference and the humour surrounding that, power, fame, the ordinariness of two extraordinary people, very little about football.

CAMERON *picks up a football, throws it around a couple of times and then places it idly at his feet. He does a couple of kick-ups before it falls. He tries a trick and almost falls over… in the middle of which* BECKHAM *walks in.*

CAMERON. David, hello! Caught me red-handed, red-footed rather, just seeing if I could still do some of the old tricks. Great to see you again, how are you?

BECKHAM. I'm good thanks, yeah.

CAMERON. You're looking good. Very fit.

BECKHAM. Yeah, well… I do my best. Doesn't get any easier.

CAMERON. Tell me about it. So you flew over in your own…

BECKHAM. Yeah. Easier really.

CAMERON. Yes. (*Beat.*) How's the family?

BECKHAM. They're good, very good.

CAMERON. Excellent. You've got the three now, haven't you? Brooklyn, Cruz and… Elvis?

BECKHAM. Romeo.

CAMERON. Romeo, sorry.

BECKHAM. Yeah. After the character by Shakespeare?

CAMERON. Right.

BECKHAM. Number Four on the way.

CAMERON. Really? Congratulations. Keep going and you'll have your own team.

BECKHAM. Yeah. What about yours?

CAMERON. Fine. Arthur, Florence and Eleanor. All thriving. We should get them together some time. They could all… (*Beat.*) you know…

BECKHAM. Yeah.

Pause.

CAMERON. So, all set for tomorrow?

BECKHAM. Yeah, I hope so. Bit of, you know, work to do.

CAMERON. Just a bit, yes, but hey, that's why we're here.

BECKHAM. Am I in the right room only…

CAMERON. Oh sorry. This is *your* room, is it? I'm so sorry, I didn't realise… no, there's been a bit of a mix-up. I've been parked here temporarily while they try and sort it out but I'll get out of your way. […] they seem to have got us down as sharing a room somehow.

BECKHAM. Tabloids will love that.

CAMERON. Wouldn't they just. You're alright with a twin then, are you?

BECKHAM. Not fussed really. So long as there's a bed and a bath. […] You still play a bit though, do you?

CAMERON. If only. Don't have the time, I'm afraid. I've also got two left feet which doesn't help.

BECKHAM. Two left feet?

CAMERON. Not literally, no! No, that would be… Anyhow, here we all are or will be shortly. Listen, I don't have to tell you that… […]

BECKHAM. Do you mind if I unpack some of this stuff? Only you want it on hangers as soon as you can else it creases up.

CAMERON. Please do. (*Looking at* BECKHAM'S *three large suitcases.*) Blimey. Sure you've brought enough clothes?

BECKHAM. Should be alright. We're only here one night, aren't we?

BECKHAM *takes something carefully out of the first suitcase and puts it to one side.*

CAMERON. What are those?

BECKHAM. Crystals.

CAMERON. Oh right.

BECKHAM. Yeah. Pink quartz and black tourmaline? Very lucky.

CAMERON. Well. I'm not going to argue with that. I suspect we're going to need all the luck we can get.

BECKHAM's *mobile phone rings.*

BECKHAM (*on phone*). Hello, babe. (*Beat.*) Yeah, about a half-hour ago… (*Beat.*) No, I'm hanging them up now… (*Beat.*) It's alright… (*Beat.*) Single bed, yeah, it's a twin, actually… (*Beat.*) I didn't ask for it… (*Beat.*) No one!… No one, I'm telling you. Well, there is someone as it happens right now but… (*Beat.*) No… no it's not actually… listen then:

He holds up the phone towards CAMERON.

Say something, will you.

CAMERON. What?

BECKHAM. Doesn't matter what, just speak.

CAMERON. Hello. David Cameron here.

BECKHAM *puts the phone back to his ear.*

BECKHAM (*on phone*). See? Male. (*Beat.*) David Cameron. (*Beat.*) The Prime Minister? (*Beat.*) England. Listen, babe, I've got to go. (*Beat.*) No, not yet. I haven't even seen him yet... (*Beat.*) Well, I can't just like, ask him, can I... (*Beat.*) I will yeah... promise... alright, love ya. Bye. (*To* CAMERON.) Bloody hell. She's desperate to get an invite to the Royal Wedding. Don't give a damn about the World Cup.

He starts taking clothes out of the suitcase and carrying them through into the bedroom. CAMERON wanders over to the window.

CAMERON. Of course, they're all in the Baur au Lac Hotel. The FIFA crowd. £2,400 a suite. Who would have thought one little duck-house and a moat could do so much damage.

BECKHAM (*off*). This is alright. I've been in worse.

He comes back in, holding a suit.

Now I thought this would do for the first meeting tonight, yeah?

CAMERON. Oh right. Yes. A suit seems... suitable.

BECKHAM. And then the second meeting, I thought maybe same kind of thing but in blue and a much narrower lapel... if I can find it. Obviously a bit more Euro, bit more, you know...

A text comes through on BECKHAM's phone.

Woah... Guess what.

CAMERON. What?

BECKHAM (*reading*). Ronaldo has had to pull out of the Spanish–Portuguese bid. Twisted his ankle.

CAMERON. Oh, that is bad luck.

BECKHAM. Yeah.

They catch each other's eye and start to laugh/celebrate.

CAMERON. Now now. Enough of that.

BECKHAM (*more text has come through*). Ladbrokes have lengthened their odds from five to two to eleven to four.

CAMERON. Have they now!

The Wardrobe

Sam Holcroft

☞ **WHO**   Martin, and Robert, both child labourers.

☞ **WHERE**   Inside the wardrobe of a child's bedroom of the Hughes family house, Liverpool.

☞ **WHEN**   9th July 1827.

☞ **WHAT HAS JUST HAPPENED**   The play is made up of twelve scenes set at different historical points, telling the stories of children and young people who have sought refuge inside the same wardrobe's thick walls. In the duologue that follows, Robert has caught Martin stealing. He drags him into the wardrobe, slamming the door shut.

☞ **WHAT TO CONSIDER**

- This scene takes place towards the end of the Industrial Revolution. In her introduction to the scene, Sam Holcroft writes: 'During the years of the Industrial Revolution, as manufacture in Britain transitions from hand-production methods to machines, children as young as four are employed in factories with dangerous and often fatal working conditions. By the early-nineteenth century, England has more than one million child workers who make up fifteen per cent of the labour force.'

- The characters are competitive with one another. There is humour in this, but we never lose sight of the real and actual suffering such children were forced to endure.

- To what extent do the children manage their pain by turning their suffering into this game of one-upmanship?

- The wardrobe is a place of escape from the outside world. Not only is it a form of physical protection, it enables the characters to express themselves freely, openly and without fear of judgement.

- This scene takes place nearly two hundred years ago, but today in other parts of the world child labour continues.

☞ WHAT MARTIN WANTS

- To plead his innocence.
- For Robert to release him.

☞ WHAT ROBERT WANTS

- To do his duty to the house but also to protect Martin. To what extent does this conflict of interests trouble him?

☞ WHAT THE SCENE IS ABOUT   The horrors of child labour, protection, survival.

☞ NB   This play offers a number of other duologues from which to choose.

The doors to the wardrobe open and ROBERT *drags* MARTIN *inside, slamming the door shut.* MARTIN *carries a lit ship's lantern, which he uses to light the chimney for cleaning.*

MARTIN. Get off me!

ROBERT. Get in there.

MARTIN. I weren't going to –

ROBERT. Keep yer voice down.

MARTIN (*more quietly*). I weren't going to take it. I were just lookin' at it.

ROBERT. You were just lookin' at it?

MARTIN. It were really shiny.

ROBERT. It were really shiny. Ain't nobody taught you how to lie better 'an that?

MARTIN. I ain't lying. I just, I just wanted to touch one of 'em. What's a person need that many teaspoons for anyhow? All lined up on display like that.

ROBERT. For eating jelly. That's right, they all congregate en masse and eat jelly.

MARTIN (*scratching*). What's 'en masse'.

ROBERT. It's French. For all together.

MARTIN (*scratching*). I ain't never spoke no French before.

ROBERT. Well, consider yourself... educated. Now, your master'll come lookin' for yer any minute, so you best get... You haven't got fleas, have yer?

MARTIN (*showing him the bites*). I got bites the size of pennies all the way up me leg. Look. You ain't seen nothing like it?

ROBERT (*looking*). Call 'em bites? I'll show you a bite. (*Lifting his trouser leg.*) Rat bite. Afore I worked in the main house I worked up the mill. Slept thirteen boys to one room. Bottom bunk weren't so much a bunk as the floor. Floor's crawling with 'em at night.

MARTIN. How do I know that ain't just a scar?

ROBERT. Cos I'm telling you it's a bite. You want a scar, I'll show you a scar. (*Pulling open his shirt collar to reveal scars around his neck.*) One morning I was late for work and the master made me wear weights round me neck and walk the length of the mill up and down. Each time I fell he added more weight.

MARTIN (*pulling up his shirt to reveal welts on his back*). Once I was late for work and the master beat me with his leather belt strap. See? That's where he caught me with the buckle.

ROBERT. That ain't worth a fart in a whirlwind. Look at this. (*Shows* MARTIN *patches of bald scalp.*) One night they left the doors unlocked. I made it as far as a field of pigs. I gorged on pig-feed. The master caught me, held me head on a bench and cut me hair off at the scalp with a meat cleaver; he took great chunks of skin. The hair ain't never grown back. And yer know what I says to him? I said, 'May the fleas of a thousand stray cats find your crotch, and may your arms be too short to scratch!' For a week he dragged me naked from my bed and made me join the assembly line holding me clothes.

MARTIN *rolls up the sleeve of his shirt to reveal suppurating skin wounds on his elbows.* ROBERT *reels back in disgust.*

MARTIN. Comes from pressing your arms against the sides of the chimney, that way I can hold my body suspended, knees and elbows pressed against the walls, it peels the skin and the soot gets in, all different kinds of soot and that causes the festerin' – (*Rolling shirt higher.*) Look, takes weeks, sometimes months to heal.

ROBERT. I lost two teeth when I passed out on the stone floor from tiredness. We hardly got a wink of sleep, starting at five in the morning.

MARTIN. I start at four.

ROBERT. Six days a week, one meal a day.

MARTIN. Once I were so hungry I ate acorns.

ROBERT. Once I were so hungry I ate a turnip frozen out of the ground.

MARTIN. Once I were so hungry I ate cabbage.

ROBERT. What's wrong with cabbage?

MARTIN. I hate cabbage.

ROBERT. Once I were so hungry I was feeling faint while cleaning the loom that I didn't hear the man shouting for me to crawl out. He let go the brake and the carriage swung back into place and crushed me arm. I managed to pull it free, but I paid the price with two of me fingers.

ROBERT *shows* MARTIN *his deformed arm and fingers.*

I were bleedin' all over the floor, and the blood were mixing with the cotton dust. It were like a field of red snow.

MARTIN. Once I were working too slowly up the chimney and Master Brindley lights a fire underneath me. Sure made me work quicker. I was dislodging so much soot that it was falling all over me and filling me pockets and getting me wedged. I was calling and begging Brindley to put the fire out, but he were asleep in the yard. The heat melted me three toes together afore a housemaid heard me screaming and fetched a bucket of water and threw it on the flames.

MARTIN *shows* ROBERT *his deformed toes.*

Now he doesn't light a fire but strips me naked and sends another boy up behind me with pins to prick the soles of me feet. (*Showing the soles of his feet.*) See? And me buttocks.

MARTIN *attempts to remove his trousers to show* ROBERT *his buttocks.*

ROBERT. S'all right, I believe you. I believe you.

MARTIN *smiles, thinking he's won the competition.*

A few pins, eh? You should consider yourself lucky. To punish me for losing me toes, the master put a nail through me ear. (*Offering his ear for inspection.*)

MARTIN *draws near.*

What happened to your eye?

MARTIN. Oh, I forgot. Once the master sent me up a chimney to get a stuck bird. It were a pigeon. Me mother says pigeons are just rats with wings. But this one were small, and delicate, and so frightened. She kept flying towards the light but her wings were so heavy with soot. I tried to take hold of her, gentle as I could, but she took fright and clawed at me forehead. She nearly took me eye. I couldn't see for a blood blister the size of a conker.

ROBERT. What happened to the bird?

MARTIN *stands and prepares to leave.*

Sorry, I weren't trying to upset yer –

MARTIN. I weren't trying to hurt 'er. And I weren't trying to steal 'em spoons. I earn my money. I been up them chimneys since I were six. That's four years. Every time me mother sees me come home with a coin in me hand she cries – big pearl-like tears hanging off 'er eyelashes. Every Sunday we eat meat, and I know I earned my share.

ROBERT. I weren't trying to –

MARTIN. Why do I need to explain meself? For all I know, you made the whole thing up. I bet yer just a serving boy who slept his whole life in a bed with feather pillows, serving jelly with silver teaspoons to rich folk in fine houses.

MARTIN *makes to leave.*

ROBERT. When I were five me father sold me to the mill as a pauper apprentice. He told me I'd be transformed into a gentleman. He told me I'd eat roast beef and Yorkshire pudding. He told me I'd have money stuffed deep into me pockets. Me first meal was cold milk–porridge of a very green complexion and me first night I had me first beating 'cause I wouldn't stop crying. When I crushed me arm I was no use to the master no more. He would've turned me out, but as it happened the landowner passed away and his son, Sir Jaffrey, inherited the estate. There were a slave who worked here. He were released according to the landowner's wishes, so they were in need of an errand boy. So here I am. Upon me honour that's the truth.

MARTIN. I believe yer.

ROBERT. I believe yer weren't trying to steal a spoon.

They smile at one another.

You best get back.

MARTIN *turns to leave; he hesitates.*

MARTIN. I know thieving is a sin. But just one silver spoon and I need never climb another chimney again.

The boys look at one another. MARTIN *jumps from the wardrobe;* ROBERT *follows close after.*

Yen

Anna Jordan

☞ **WHO**   Brothers Bobbie, thirteen, and Hench, sixteen.

☞ **WHERE**   The living room (which has been turned into a bedroom) in their flat on an estate in Feltham, Greater London.

☞ **WHEN**   Present day. 10 p.m.

☞ **WHAT HAS JUST HAPPENED**   Hench and his younger brother Bobbie live on their own in a grotty flat on a run-down estate. Their mother is an alcoholic, who shows up occasionally, mostly drunk and when she needs stuff from the flat to sell. Otherwise the boys fend for themselves. They spend most of their time watching hard-core pornography and playing violent games on their PlayStation. They have a pet dog called Taliban who never goes out, and is shut up in the bedroom where he shits and pees. In the meantime a strange girl has been watching Taliban from across the road where she can see him in the upstairs window. The following duologue forms the start of the play. Bobbie is watching the girl – the 'skank' – and Hench is watching porn on a laptop linked to the TV.

☞ **WHAT TO CONSIDER**

- Despite the harshness of their upbringing and their time spent playing violent games and watching porn, Hench and Bobbie are highly sensitive, caring and sweet. At no point does the playwright judge or dismiss them.

- Read the play to find out what happens when the strange girl makes herself known.

- As we will discover the title of the play is the strange girl's nickname. Her parents were relatively old when they had her and the word 'yen' describes the longing with which she was conceived.

- All the play's characters are in a state of longing for a love they have not known.

- The sensory nature of the scene. From the Lucozade to the Lynx, it is abundant with strong tastes and smells.

- The opening stage direction is much longer in the published playscript. I recommend reading it to get a full picture of how the boys are living.

☞ WHAT BOBBIE WANTS

- To be close to Hench.

- To be part of a family. (He is desperate for his mother to arrive.)

- To feel safe.

☞ WHAT HENCH WANTS

- To protect Bobbie. Notice how he attempts to keep him in check.

- To love and to be loved.

☞ WHAT THE SCENE IS ABOUT   Survival, brotherly love, longing, need.

A living room which has been made into a bedroom. Everything is tatty and worn, apart from a collection of shiny equipment: a flat-screen TV, PlayStation, laptop and some speakers. HENCH *and* BOBBIE *are watching hardcore pornography linked from the laptop to the TV by HDMI.* BOBBIE *leans down by the side of the bed and comes back with a pint of milk in a glass bottle. He downs quite a lot of it and does a little burp after. He puts the milk down and runs over to a window. He looks out.*

BOBBIE. She's still there.

HENCH. Is it?

BOBBIE. Yeah.

> HENCH *glances briefly towards the window, and then back to the TV.*

> What a skank.

> Hench?

Beat. Nothing from HENCH. BOBBIE *leans out of the window.*

Piss off, you skank! –

HENCH. Shhhh, man! You'll wake the dog.

Beat.

BOBBIE. What does she want?

HENCH. I dunno, do I?

BOBBIE. Maybe she wants to fuck you.

HENCH. Fuck off.

BOBBIE (*looking out*). She's got reeeeaaaaalllly small tits, man! I need a sniper scope just to see 'em. (*Beat.*) Hench?

No response from HENCH. BOBBIE *runs towards the bed and jumps on it three times, annoying* HENCH. *Then he flops down next to him and looks at the screen.*

Not like those, bruv. (*Pointing.*) One of those is bigger than your head.

HENCH. They're fake innit.

BOBBIE. *Is* it?

HENCH. Yeah!

Beat. BOBBIE *ponders this.*

BOBBIE. I would want a girlfriend with fake tits.

BOBBIE *rests his chin on* HENCH's *shoulder.*

HENCH. Get off, man.

BOBBIE (*still watching*). Can a *man's* arsehole go like that?

HENCH. Like what?

BOBBIE. All big, like that?

He makes a circle with his hands.

HENCH. S'pose.

BOBBIE. Oh my DAYS!

HENCH (*irritated*). A man's arsehole can basically do whatever a woman's arsehole can do innit?

BOBBIE. *Is* it?

HENCH. Yeah! How do you think gays do it?

BOBBIE. Gays are dirty.

HENCH. Yep.

BOBBIE. I fucking hate gays. (*Beat. Thinks.*) Do you think my arsehole would do that?

HENCH. DON'T even think about it!

Beat. BOBBIE *runs round in front of* HENCH.

BOBBIE. Can you scratch my back?

HENCH. No. MOVE.

BOBBIE. But I got an itch! And it's a bitch! (*Thinks for a sec.*) Oi. Hench. (*Like Jay Z.*) 'I got ninety-nine problems but an itch ain't one!'

HENCH *picks up a large bottle of Lucozade from the side of the bed and has a swig.*

Don't drink the Lucozade!

HENCH. She's not coming!

BOBBIE. In case she does though and she needs it.

HENCH. She's all loved-up with Minge-Face Alan. Rolling his fags. Washing his socks. And you know what they smell like.

BOBBIE. Like sick.

HENCH. 'Xactly. So she ain't coming, is she?

Beat. BOBBIE *looks sad.*

She never washed our fucking socks.

BOBBIE. We haven't got any socks.

HENCH. We used to.

Beat.

BOBBIE. She might want a break from it all.

HENCH. What and you reckon she'd come here? It's hardly a Premier fucking Inn, is it?

BOBBIE. What if she comes round and goes low and has a hypo and DIES cos we've got nothing to give her! That would be you then, that would, you would have *killed* our mother.

Beat. HENCH *sighs and puts the Lucozade down.*

Ah fanks, bro. Here.

BOBBIE *fetches the bottle of half-drunk milk from the side of the bed.*

Have some milk.

HENCH. I don't want your fucking milk, do I? What d'you nick milk for?

BOBBIE. It was off a doorstep. (*Beat.*) Might make you stronger.

HENCH. Fuck off.

Beat. BOBBIE *thinks. To make amends he runs up to the window. He pulls his trousers down and presses his bare bottom against the glass.*

BOBBIE. HENCH!

No response from HENCH.

Hench. Bruv. LOOK!

HENCH *glances.* BOBBIE *turns back and looks out of the window.*

Oh.

He wanders back to the sofa bed but doesn't sit.

She's gone. She was waiting for you.

HENCH. You should show her your shrivelled little cock. Then she'd go and never come back.

BOBBIE *slaps* HENCH *around the back of the head.* HENCH *jumps up.*

Don't fucking hit me, right? I told you not to hit me!

HENCH *gets* BOBBIE *in a headlock. They struggle.*

Suddenly BOBBIE *begins to bark viciously at* HENCH. HENCH *stumbles back and knocks the Lucozade over.*

BOBBIE. The LUCOZADE!

He goes to rescue it.

HENCH. You're a fucking animal.

Suddenly a dog starts barking for real, loud and aggressive, from the other room.

Now look what you've done, prick. Shut *UP*, TALIBAN!

He pushes BOBBIE *towards the door.*

Right, you're going in with him!

BOBBIE. I can't – we got no food for him!

HENCH. Well, you should have thought of that, shouldn't you?? Prick.

He kicks BOBBIE *hard in the arse and* BOBBIE *skids a bit. A stand-off. The dog stops barking now. Calm descends for a moment.* HENCH *sits back down.*

You stink.

BOBBIE. You're ugly.

HENCH. Your pits, man. And your hair. And your breath. You stink like rotten milk. Go brush your teeth.

BOBBIE. I haven't got a toothbrush.

HENCH. What you been using then?

BOBBIE. Yours.

HENCH lunges for BOBBIE *and* BOBBIE *hops away, laughing gleefully.*

HA! Just jokes, bruvva! Just jokes innit.

HENCH. Fuck you. Have a wash.

BOBBIE. Oi. You're Hench. I'm Stench. Gettit?

BOBBIE wanders over to the shelf, grabs a can of Lynx and sprays it liberally under his arms. He hovers it over his open tracksuit bottoms.

Hench.

No response from HENCH. *He sprays it liberally into his shorts. Then he sprays his hair. Then he sprays into his mouth and starts to cough.* HENCH *ignores him. He wanders back over to the screen.*

Oh, snap! Look how far his cum shoots out of his dick, bruv! Does yours go that far?

HENCH. Shut up.

BOBBIE. We should have a competition.

HENCH. Fuck off.

BOBBIE. If you could cum on any part of woman, where would it be?

HENCH. Dunno.

BOBBIE. Come on. Think!

HENCH. Tits I guess.

BOBBIE. I'd cum in her eyes. Blind the bitch.

Beat. BOBBIE *loses interest in the video and starts wandering the room. He picks up an old T-shirt from the floor, puts it on.*

I'm *hungry*, bruv. I feel like I got a monster in me tummy. Are there any Wheat Crunchies left?

HENCH. You gave the last bag to Taliban.

BOBBIE (*in a cod-American accent*). Oh, *man*!

HENCH. There's Twiglets.

BOBBIE. Twiglets???

HENCH. Yeah.

BOBBIE. Twiglets taste like your arsehole. (*Beat. Has an idea.*) And they look like your dick!

HENCH. WELL, DON'T FUCKING EAT THEM THEN!

BOBBIE. Ooh, alright, don't have a period! Jeeezus.

HENCH (*slamming the laptop shut*). I'm going to bed.

BOBBIE. What about COD?

HENCH. What about it?

BOBBIE. We was gonna have a night sesh! Fuck up those – (*In a cod-American accent.*) American faggots.

HENCH. You do my head in, Bobbie.

HENCH *turns the light off.*

BOBBIE. What if I want it on?

HENCH. Tough shit.

BOBBIE. Oh, *brother*!

HENCH *takes his jeans off and gets into bed.*

You're not sleeping in your pants, are you? What if your horrible cock escapes and touches me in the night?

HENCH *throws a pillow at* BOBBIE. BOBBIE *giggles. He opens the laptop. The porn noise starts again.*

HENCH. Switch it off.

BOBBIE. I wanna watch it.

HENCH. Put it on mute then!

BOBBIE. Oh. It's no fun without the noises.

BOBBIE *puts it on mute. He carefully puts it down in front of him. He sits at the end of the bed, the screen lighting his face.* BOBBIE *turns round to check behind him, then puts his hand down his tracksuit bottoms and starts wanking a little bit inside them.*

Pause. Calm descends for a moment, just a little twitching noise. Suddenly HENCH *sits upright in bed.*

HENCH. BOBBIE, STOP WANKING!

BOBBIE *jumps with shock and then shows him both hands.*

BOBBIE. I wasn't! I swear. Go to sleep!

HENCH *lies back down.* BOBBIE *dissolves into a fit of giggles.*

Your face, bruv.

'STOP WANKING.'

'BOBBIE, STOP WANKING.'

He giggles. He sniffs his fingers. Thinks about sticking them under HENCH's *nose. Thinks better of it.*

Goodnight, brother. Dream about that skank.

www.nickhernbooks.co.uk

facebook.com/nickhernbooks

twitter.com/nickhernbooks